Cambridge Elements

Elements in Development Economics
Series Editor-in-Chief
Kunal Sen
UNU-WIDER and University of Manchester

POVERTY IN LATIN AMERICA

Feelings/Perceptions vs Material Conditions

Verónica Amarante
University of the Republic

Maira Colacce
University of the Republic

Federico Scalese
University of the Republic

Shaftesbury Road, Cambridge CB2 8EA, United Kingdom

One Liberty Plaza, 20th Floor, New York, NY 10006, USA

477 Williamstown Road, Port Melbourne, VIC 3207, Australia

314–321, 3rd Floor, Plot 3, Splendor Forum, Jasola District Centre,
New Delhi – 110025, India

103 Penang Road, #05–06/07, Visioncrest Commercial, Singapore 238467

Cambridge University Press is part of Cambridge University Press & Assessment,
a department of the University of Cambridge.

We share the University's mission to contribute to society through the pursuit of
education, learning and research at the highest international levels of excellence.

www.cambridge.org
Information on this title: www.cambridge.org/9781009542043

DOI: 10.1017/9781009542036

First published 2025

A catalogue record for this publication is available from the British Library

ISBN 978-1-009-54204-3 Hardback
ISBN 978-1-009-54206-7 Paperback
ISSN 2755-1601 (online)
ISSN 2755-1598 (print)

Poverty in Latin America

Feelings/Perceptions vs Material Conditions

Elements in Development Economics

DOI: 10.1017/9781009542036
First published online: May 2025

Verónica Amarante
University of the Republic

Maira Colacce
University of the Republic

Federico Scalese
University of the Republic

Author for correspondence: Verónica Amarante,
veronica.amarante@fcea.edu.uy

Abstract: This Element derives subjective poverty lines (SPL) for seven Latin American countries based on a minimum income question (MIQ) included in household expenditure surveys. It compares poverty incidence under the subjective and objective approach, finding subjective poverty is larger than objective for all countries. People identified as poor are generaly poor by both measures or only subjective poor, although patterns of overlapping differ between countries. It explores the factors associated to considering oneself as poor – being subjectively poor – when the per capita household income is higher than the objective poverty line. Generaly, unemployment and informality are associated with higher probability of subjective poverty. Other factors not directly involving income but reflecting high economic security also tend to reduce the probability of feeling poor. Finally, the welfare stigma effect does not seem to hold, at least in terms of subjective poverty. This title is also available as Open Access on Cambridge Core.

Keywords: poverty lines, subjective poverty, Latin America, material conditions, feelings

JEL classifications: I32, O10

ISBNs: 9781009542043 (HB), 9781009542067 (PB), 9781009542036 (OC)
ISSNs: 2755-1601 (online), 2755-1598 (print)

Contents

1 Introduction

Fighting poverty consists of one of the main objectives of any development agenda. The importance of this goal has led to refinement in the measurement of deprivation, with a central role of household income or consumption to reflect household's well-being. The development of objective measures to reflect poverty based on monetary metrics has been profuse in the economic literature, as well as the discussion about its limitations (Ravallion, 2016). This approach also has a long tradition in Latin American countries (Altimir, 1981; Gasparini et al., 2013; ECLAC, 2019; among others).[1]

On a somehow parallel path, scholars have attempted to measure subjective well-being based on respondent's self-assessments in survey questions. A popular approach to collecting subjective data on poverty consists of asking for a money-metric of subjective welfare. As in the objective approach, the underlying assumption is that it is possible to make interindividual welfare comparisons on the poverty/non-poverty threshold. The most widely used approach is based on the minimum income question (MIQ) that asks what income level does the person consider to be absolutely minimal, in the sense that with less she or he could not make ends meet (see among others, Goedhart et al., 1977; Van Praag et al., 1980; Danziger et al., 1984; De Vos & Garner, 1991).[2] Theses subjective questions are used to calibrate an interpersonally comparable welfare function based on observed covariates which are assumed to be relevant (Ravallion, 2010). Potential limitations of subjective measures arise from response errors, random discrepancies in the interpretation of the survey questions, idiosyncratic differences in the respondents' moods, and differences in tastes and personality, among others.

Efforts to integrate the subjective and objective approaches, based on the idea that income-based objective welfare indicators may fail to account for important socioeconomic factors that could affect the level of a household's well-being, have found relatively higher levels of aggregate poverty under the subjective approach. They have also detected significant differences in the poverty profiles derived from these measures (Ravallion & Lokshin, 2002; Lokshin et al., 2006). This divergence may hide relevant information for our understanding of poverty. More specifically, objective poverty lines often imply that larger households are poorer, but this is not typically the case in studies

---

[1] Objective measures based on the multidimensional approach (Alkire & Foster, 2007, 2011) are also relevant for the poverty debate in the region (see Santos & Villatoro, 2018).

[2] Other approaches use qualitative categories in the welfare space, for example, based on the economic ladder question, or on broader concepts such as satisfaction with life or happiness (see Van Praag & Ferrer-i-Carbonell, 2004) as well as consumption adequacy questions (Pradhan and Ravallion, 2000; Lokshin et al., 2006).

under the subjective approach, which implies greater economies of scale than normally assumed (Ravallion, 2010).

In Latin America, the tradition of poverty measurement has been based on the comparison of objective absolute poverty lines with income data obtained from household surveys. The pioneering work of Altimir (1979, 1981) set the grounds for the measurement of the cost of basic food and nonfood needs, and at present most countries in the region calculate their own official poverty indicators using objective absolute poverty lines. Although poverty has been at the center of the region's research agenda for many years (Amarante et al., 2018), subjective poverty has not been widely addressed. Some studies have considered the welfare-relevant information contained in subjective measures (Herrera, 2002; Luchetti, 2006; Rojas & Jiménez, 2008; Scalese, 2022), but comparative analysis at the country level remains missing.

This Element examines the economic foundations of objective and subjective approaches to poverty measurement, focusing on seven Latin American countries: Brazil, Colombia, Ecuador, El Salvador, Paraguay, Peru, and Uruguay. We estimate household-specific subjective poverty lines (SPL) for each country and analyze the overlap between objective and subjective poverty identification methods. For each country, we compare poverty profiles derived from both objective and subjective thresholds. It is important to note that our primary analysis is based on national objective poverty lines and national SPLs, which are not directly comparable across countries. Consequently, we do not conduct cross-country comparisons of poverty levels. However, for robustness purposes, we also consider comparable objective poverty lines calculated by the Economic Commission for Latin America and the Caribbean (ECLAC) and also the ones proposed by the World Bank.

Our study contributes novel empirical evidence to the field of poverty research in several key aspects. It provides one of the first systematic comparisons of subjective and objective poverty measures across multiple Latin American countries, filling an important gap in the regional literature. By using recent data and rigorous methodologies to estimate SPLs, we contribute to the understanding of how individuals in different contexts perceive their economic needs. We examine the overlap and divergences between subjective and objective poverty measures, shedding light on the factors that may influence discrepancies between these measures. Our analysis of how household characteristics and broader economic conditions may affect perceptions of poverty provides insights into the determinants of subjective poverty. By considering both national and internationally comparable poverty lines, we offer a nuanced perspective on how different thresholds may affect poverty measurement. Furthermore, we explore the implications of our findings for policy formulation, suggesting how the integration of subjective and objective measures could inform more effective poverty-reduction strategies.

Additionally, we reflect on the implications of incorporating subjective poverty measurements into broader poverty discussions and the design of poverty alleviation policies. In doing so, this study seeks to contribute to a more informed debate about the multifaceted nature of poverty and how it can be most effectively measured and addressed in the Latin American context.

This Element offers several methodological contributions. We employ a rigorous approach to estimating SPLs, building on and extending previous work in this area. Our use of household-specific SPLs illustrates how perceptions of poverty vary across different household types and socioeconomic contexts. Furthermore, our comparative analysis across seven countries provides insights into how the relationship between subjective and objective poverty measures may vary in different national contexts.

From a theoretical perspective, our study contributes to ongoing debates about the nature of poverty and how it should be conceptualized and measured. By examining the divergences between subjective and objective measures, we shed light on the complex relationship between material deprivation and perceived economic well-being. This analysis has implications for how we understand the multidimensional nature of poverty and the potential limitations of relying solely on income-based measures.

The remainder of this Element is structured as follows: Section 2 provides a comprehensive discussion of objective and subjective approaches to poverty measurement, examining their theoretical foundations, comparative advantages, and limitations. Section 3 addresses the methodological considerations in establishing objective and SPLs. Section 4 synthesizes the existing literature on subjective poverty, with particular emphasis on Latin American studies. Section 5 outlines our data sources and methodological framework. Section 6 presents a comparative analysis of subjective and objective poverty measures across the seven countries in our study. Section 7 examines the discrepancies between objective and subjective poverty measurements and investigates their underlying determinants. Section 8 explores the relationship between consumption patterns and subjective poverty. Finally, Section 9 concludes with policy implications and directions for future research.

By providing a comprehensive analysis of subjective and objective poverty measures in Latin America, this study aims to contribute to a more nuanced understanding of poverty in the region and to inform more effective poverty-reduction strategies. Our findings have implications not only for academic debates about poverty measurement but also for policymakers seeking to design and implement more targeted and effective anti-poverty programs.

2 Objective and Subjective Approaches to Poverty

2.1 Objective Approach

Poverty alleviation is a concern shared by various social actors, including academics, and the identification of people living in poverty becomes crucial to think about the design and implementation of policies aimed at this end. With this objective in mind, a relevant step is the identification of people living in poverty. Academic debates on this subject have a long history, dating back to the late nineteenth century and the discussion about how to reflect the insufficiency of income to cover basic needs for the fulfillment of mere physical efficiency. This early approach is founded on the idea of objectivity, implying that there is a certain reality which can be captured by a specific measure. Poverty is confined to the material aspects of life and a monetary metric is needed to reflect the phenomenon. The origins of this approach can be traced to the contributions of Booth and Rowentree, who documented the living conditions of England's poor in the cities of London and York during the late nineteenth and early twentieth centuries.

This is still the approach with the largest development in economics (Ravallion, 2010) and allows for multiple non-income dimensions of welfare, reflecting an absolute view in the space of welfare. The formalization of the approach assumes a utility function for individual i of the form $u(q_i, x_i)$, where q_i is a vector of the quantities of commodities consumed and x_i is a vector of non-income characteristics which are relevant for welfare, including demographic characteristics of the household. The utility maximizing consumption vector is denoted $q(p_i, y_i, x_i)$ at price vector p_i and total expenditure on consumption y_i. The implied indirect utility function is $v(p_i, y_i, x_i)$, which gives the maximum attainable welfare at the prevailing prices and characteristics and can be inverted to get the expenditure function $e(p_i, y_i, x_i)$. This function gives the minimum cost of utility u for person i when facing prices p_i.

If the minimum utility necessary to escape poverty is denoted u_z, the welfare consistent poverty lines are given by $z_i^u = e(p_i, x_i, u_z)$, which can in turn be rewritten as $z_i^u = p_i q^c(p_i, x_i, u_z)$. This equation reflects that the welfare consistent poverty line is the cost of a bundle of basic consumption needs given by the vector of utility-compensated demands at the reference level of utility defining who is poor in the welfare space. The poverty rate is then the proportion of population whose income[3] is below the poverty line, $\frac{y_i}{z_i^u} \leq 1$. In other words, a

---

[3] The monetary aggregate for poverty measures is generally income or consumption. Latin American countries' tradition of poverty measurement is based on income, as in developed countries. In general terms, the rest of the developing world uses expenditure for poverty measurement. In this Element, we refer to income, as we focus on Latin American countries.

person is identified as poor if their household income is below a certain monetary threshold. At present, most absolute poverty thresholds reflect an income level that covers not only the minimum nutritional requirements for good health and a normal level of activity but also the goods and services that cover other needs.

It is important to notice that this framework allows for a measure of absolute monetary poverty, as the one undertaken in this study, but it is also consistent with relative monetary poverty measurement, and with the measurement of nonmonetary poverty. These three measures (absolute, relative, and nonmonetary) are part of the objective approach to poverty measurement.[4] In the case of relative income, it is possible to assume that the vector of non-income characteristics which are relevant for welfare, x_i, includes mean income of some reference group.

Moreover, Ravallion (2010) has argued that the objective framework is consistent with the measurement of poverty as deprivation in terms of a persons' functionings, as proposed by Sen's (1985) influential work. This would imply considering that poverty is the situation of not having sufficient income to support specific normative functionings. Nevertheless, most studies of deprivation under the capability approach have taken alternative paths, considering multidimensional deprivation based on the Alkire–Foster multidimensional counting approach (Alkire & Foster, 2007, 2011). This implies identifying the multidimensionally poor based on a two-stage process in which a threshold is defined for deprivation in each dimension and then a second cutoff is established to determine the number of dimensions in which someone is required to be deprived to be identified as multidimensionally poor. None of these two stages implies the consideration of equivalent income to fulfill a certain functioning.

As discussed, the measure of poverty through a monetary-based method can be built upon an absolute or a relative poverty line. The absolute poverty line is set in reference to the cost of a basic food basket plus a given sum for covering nonfood needs, referring to certain elements required to survive, such as clothing or shelter. The alternative is to use a relative poverty line that is set based on the comparison with a reference group. In general, this is defined with reference to a certain point in the income or expenditure distribution. For instance, European countries use this approach and consider the poverty line as equivalent to 60 percent of median equivalized household income.

In any case, the objective approach is based on the idea that poverty is confined to material aspects of life and can be measured based on information

---

[4] It is also theoretically possible to address subjective poverty based on an absolute, relative, or non monetary approach.

about these aspects. The differences within this approach are on whether the command is over commodities or over what an individual can and cannot do in life and on the importance of the reference group to establish the poverty threshold.

2.2 Criticisms to the Objective Approach

The objective approach to poverty implies that there is a certain reality "out there" which can be captured through certain statistical methodologies (Ruggeri Laderchi et al., 2003). The idea of being able to capture and monitor the situation of the population with regard to poverty is undoubtedly appealing. But when moving on to the action of poverty measurement, a big number of (very) relevant assumptions are needed, and this leads to questioning the claim of objectivity of the measurement. There are value judgments involved, which can be made explicit or subject to sensitivity analysis by the researchers. In any case, it is difficult to consider the measurement as purely objective and completely free of biases. In what follows, and given the scope of our study, we concentrate on the main criticisms of the objective approach to poverty based on absolute monetary poverty lines. The expert-based definition of food baskets and poverty lines has been considered as a rather paternalistic procedure to define a socially acceptable poverty line (Van Praag & Ferrer Carbonell, 2005).

It is true that the underlying assumptions are derived from economic theory, but most of these assumptions cannot be tested or evaluated. Some of the controversial aspects involved include the technical rules for the determination of food requirements, the definition of the essential consumption basket, the issue of how to price comparable goods in different regions, the treatment of different housing situations, and the adjustment of needed resources according to household size and composition. Besides all these technical aspects, the objective monetary method does not consider that household income or expenditure is endogenous to its preferences and needs (Sen, 1985). Households may prefer to reduce the hours of work if they value leisure over consumption, and this may lead to considering these households as income poor, even if they do not consider themselves poor because of their valuation of leisure.

The objective approach, based on external value judgments, completely ignores the real perception of the poor. The convenience of complementing the expert-derived poverty thresholds with views that consider the insider's perspectives and people's perceptions about their own poverty status has received significant support from academics. Among others, Deaton (2010) has underlined that people themselves have a very good idea of whether they are poor, and so their opinions should be considered. In his words, "there is

> Box 1 Objectivity in Poverty Measurement
>
> One cannot completely eliminate the value judgements inherent in the construction of poverty thresholds, we should try to make the ad hoc assumptions more justifiable. (Kakwani, 2010, p. 36)
>
> The choice of reference group should be determined on the basis of the commitment the governments want to make in terms of allocating resources to poverty reduction programs. (Kakwani, 2010, p. 39)
>
> In the end, a judgment is invariably required as to whether the implied lines seem reasonable in the specific setting. (Ravallion, 2010, p. 11)
>
> What one is doing in setting an objective poverty line in a given country is attempting to estimate the country's underlying social subjective poverty line. (Ravallion, 2010, p. 24)
>
> Importance of testing the sensitivity of poverty comparisons to the choice of reference, as it determines the level of the poverty line. (Ravallion, 2012, p. 6)
>
> There is "scope for debate at virtually every step" in generating objective poverty measures. (Ravallion & Lokshin, 2001, p. 338)

something to be said for directly asking people around the world how their lives are going, whether they have enough, or whether they are in financial difficulty, and in cases where there are reliable income data, turning those reports into poverty lines" (Deaton, 2010). A few sentences written by the most prestigious poverty researchers suffice to illustrate the simplification implied by the pretension of complete objectivity in poverty measurement (see Box 1).

2.3 Subjective Approach

A different approach to identify poverty situations consists in asking people about how they perceive their own welfare, whether in absolute or relative terms, and making subjective interpersonal welfare comparisons. In words of Ravallion (2010), this approach can be considered as an attempt of cross-fertilization between the antagonistic "objective-quantitative" and "subjective-qualitative" schools of poverty that dominate different academic disciplines. This approach is by far not the dominant one in poverty research, although in recent years some studies based on subjective information have emerged. The low prevalence of studies based on the subjective approach in economics derives, to a certain point, from the scarcity of these data. But it is also explained by economists' skepticism about whether these questions elicit meaningful answers for welfare measuring, as discussed in Section 2.3.

The subjective approach measures the welfare levels of households based on their responses to "subjective" questions about their evaluations of their own economic status, instead of deriving utility-based measures from market behavior. Then, a poverty threshold is derived in the monetary space, defined as the income level at which some critical level of subjective welfare is reached in expectation.

The departing point of the subjective approach is the theory of consumer behavior developed by Van Praag (1968), based on the idea that the individual can evaluate his welfare position with respect to their income level on a bounded scale. This approach is in the tradition of cardinal utility, as opposed to the possibility of only being able to order according to (ordinal) preferences. It allows for the derivation of an individual *welfare function of income* or cardinal utility function of income, which measures only the individual relative welfare as perceived by the individual. Each individual has his or her own individual welfare function. It is measured as a proportion between the current welfare and the welfare that could be in the optimal imaginable situation. Welfare is approximated by income and the welfare function is evaluated on a 0 to 1 scale.

The pioneering work of Van Praag (1971) and Van Praag & Kapteyn (1973) at the University of Leyden was developed within this framework, attempting to verify the operationality of the theory proposed in Van Praag (1968) and to estimate the welfare function of income for a sample of individuals. Besides the theoretical formulation, they provide empirical illustrations based on a specific question included in consumer union surveys for Belgium and the Netherlands, respectively. On theoretical grounds, individuals should be provided with a series of income levels and asked to evaluate these levels in a bounded space, for example, on a 0 to 1 scale. This is a complex exercise, as it would be very challenging for extremely poor people to discern the differences among various high-income levels (and the other way round). The solution is to employ an indirect method, using the so-called *income evaluation question*, which allows to elicit an individual's welfare judgments. Through this question, the individual is asked to determine the level of income he or she considers fits into certain categories associated to utility.

In the original work of Van Praag (1971) and Van Praag & Kapteyn (1973), the categories were "Excellent," "Good," "Amply sufficient," "Sufficient," "Barely sufficient," "Insufficient," "Very insufficient," "Bad," and "Very bad." By answering, the individual gives a division of the income range into certain intervals. The answers to this question are transformed into numbers on a 0 to 1 scale, under the assumption that the individual partitions the income range according to equal percentiles of the welfare function. This information allows to estimate the individual welfare function of income, which is represented through a lognormal distribution and whose welfare parameters μ and σ may differ between individuals. Different exercises have considered welfare levels between 0.4 and 0.6 on a 0 to 1 scale to set the poverty line (Goedhart et al., 1977; Van Praag et al., 1982). According to Van Praag et al. (1982), a level of 0.5 means approximately that a family is called poor if it evaluates its income as barely sufficient or less.

The underlying idea is that a society and its policymakers can stipulate a certain minimum welfare evaluation below which citizens should not fall. The income levels corresponding to those minimum welfare evaluation levels defines the poverty threshold. The computation of the corresponding minimum income levels for each individual in order not to fall below that minimum welfare according to their welfare function of income is straightforward and allows the estimation of national SPLs.

The other approach to build a SPL consists of asking only one income amount that corresponds to a specific welfare label, instead of asking several income levels that correspond to several welfare levels – as done through the income evaluation question. This question is called the MIQ and can be conceived as a simplified version of the income equivalent question (see Flik & Van Praag, 1991). A typical formulation of the MIQ question is: *To meet the expenses you consider necessary, what do you think is the minimum income, a family like yours needs, on a yearly/monthly basis, to make ends meet?*.[5] A similar question with an alternative wording is the minimum spending question: *In your opinion, how much would you have to spend each year/month in order to provide the basic necessities for your family?* (see Garner & Short, 2003).

The "MIQ" seeks to get the respondent to declare what the minimum income would be he or she considers necessary for his or her household to "make ends meet." Of course, the response to this question is influenced by several idiosyncratic and psychological factors, so it is not one's stated perception of own welfare that is taken to be the relevant welfare metric. Instead, the subjective question provides information for the identification of a metric of welfare, including the setting of SPLs. In sum, these subjective questions are used to calibrate an interpersonally comparable welfare function based on observed relevant covariates (Ravallion, 2010).

This implies that it is necessary to estimate a model with the answer to the MIQ as the dependent variable and the household income, together with other

---

[5] An alternative approach to MIQ consists on addressing subjective income poverty through the economic ladder question: *Imagine six steps, where on the bottom, the first step, stand the poorest people, and on the highest step, the sixth, stand the rich. On which step are you today?*

characteristics of the person or household that are considered important, as regressors. The result of the estimation is equated with the household income, to subsequently clear the value of the income that defines the SPL. Thus, all households below this line are considered poor. As underlined by Peng et al. (2020), it should be noted that although the SPL has been classified as a subjective approach, it in fact stands somewhere between the economic approach of measuring poverty by monetary indicators set by outsiders and the subjective approach of asking respondents to assess their own degree of poverty.

The "MIQ" had its first applications in the works of Goedhart et al. (1977), Van Praag et al. (1980, 1982), Danziger et al. (1984), Colasanto et al. (1984), Kapteyn et al. (1988), and De Vos & Garner (1991). In this Element, we use this strategy to build SPLs for Latin American countries. The methodological details for the estimation of SPLs are discussed in Section 3.

2.4 Criticisms to the Subjective Approach

The extent to which subjective perceptions of individuals really reflect objective social conditions is a contented issue driven and encouraged by the famous Easterlin paradox which argues that when a country's income increases, happiness does not increase (Easterlin, 1974).[6] One potential reason for this paradox is that individuals evaluate their well-being in relation to other groups or points in time, although this remains an open debate (Burchardt, 2005; Di Tella & MacCulloch, 2008; Clark, 2018).

Focusing on the more specific issue of subjective poverty measurement, critiques are also abundant. One strand of literature poses theoretical critiques to the welfare income function. Seidl (1994) questions that the utility function of income is bounded from both below and above and criticizes the idea that a utility function of money has a convex–concave form. Van Praag & Kapteyn (1994) respond to the first critique by providing counterexamples of bounded utility functions, such as those used in the literature on decisions under uncertainty (Arrow, 1971). In relation to the second critique, Van Praag & Kapteyn (1994) defend the proposal of a convex–concave or sigmoid form of the utility function, arguing that for extremely poor people, an extra dollar brings them closer to survival, implying that the utility function would be convex shaped until the individual exceeds the situation of poverty.

But most critiques refer to the underlying assumption that everyone ascribes the same welfare meaning to the concept of "minimally necessary income." If

---

[6] The literature discussing the empirical support for Easterlin paradox includes (but is not limited to) Frey & Stutzer (2002), Blanchflower & Oswald (2004), and Easterlin et al. (2010).

the answers to the MIQ s are related to differences in lifestyle and not to actual costs or needs, their use for poverty assessment is questionable. Garner & De Vos (1995) include expenditure in the estimation of the subjective thresholds and compare respondents from the United States and the Netherlands, finding that the US respondents were thinking about their current expenditures and lifestyles, rather than their "basic needs" when answering the question. This implies that the assumption that everyone adheres the same welfare connotation to a "minimally necessary income" may not be valid across surveys or between and within populations, posing a doubt about the measurement of subjective poverty. On the same line, in the case of the Leyden poverty line, it is necessary to assume that people can evaluate income levels in general and their own income in terms of "good," "bad," "sufficient," and so on. It is also assumed that the verbal labels can be translated into a utility function that is bounded on a 0 to 1 scale.

Another potential limitation is the possibility that the measure of income obtained from the survey for calculating a SPL may not be consistent with what respondents have in mind when they answer the MIQ. The method assumes that every respondent gives the same welfare meaning to the phrase "minimally necessary income," an assumption not always backed by the evidence (Garner & De Vos, 1995). The survey-based income is estimated considering many questions covering a wide range of potential sources of income, and the respondent builds his or her income by systematically considering these different sources. The MIQ assumes that the respondent already knows its income and can bring a precise response to a unique question. Additionally, households may have different concepts of income that may not correspond to the concept of income of the MIQ. Special components of income such as cash income, imputed rent, or income from own production activities are of particular concern in relation to these divergencies. Given these issues, Pradhan & Ravallion (2000) conclude that there are serious difficulties in obtaining sensible answers to the usual MIQ in most developing countries, and they propose a method to retrieve the SPL from some qualitative questions on perceived consumption adequacy added to an integrated household survey.

On the same line, if self-assessment of well-being reflects aspirations rather than real circumstances, and if these aspirations are influenced by how own's situation compares to well-being of other households, the measurement of subjective poverty may not be clear-cut.

In their discussion about the limitations of subjective data, Bertrand & Mullainathan (2001) conclude that experimental evidence supports the idea that cognitive effects (ordering of questions, wording, etc.) affect the way people answer subjective questions. This casts doubts about the use of variables originated from subjective questions as dependent variables, as measurement error seems to be correlated with characteristics and behaviors. On a similar line, Ravallion & Lokshin (2002) indicate that personality traits may influence how people respond to subjective welfare questions, so we would need to control latent psychological differences to identify welfare levels.

A more positive view about the use of subjective data and the calibration of subjective poverty measures is given by Ravallion (2010), who underlines the trade-offs between the problems inherent to subjective data and the welfare relevant information that it may contain.

3 The Definition of Objective and Subjective Poverty Lines

A poverty line represents a relevant threshold in any society and the setting of this line involves a political decision (Goedhart et al., 1977). The establishment of a poverty line implies normative options that may go beyond technical aspects. There are not internationally validated standards that can be applied in all contexts, so the setting of a poverty line invariably implies a certain degree of arbitrariness (Deaton, 1997). Moreover, the discussions and deliberations of poverty thresholds take place within the framework of historical processes and specific contexts, where national and international institutions and organizations also play an important role. The decisions made when setting the poverty threshold may have implications in terms of public policies and access to public benefits.

On economic grounds, the poverty line should reflect the costs of attaining a certain standard of living, and this minimum level of welfare can be identified based on an objective or a subjective approach, as discussed in Section 2.3. Within each approach, there is a broad set of decisions that must be made to set the line in each context, and these decisions have impact on the results obtained.

Following Ravallion (2010), the main methods found in developing countries to set *absolute poverty lines* are the food-energy intake method and the cost of basic needs method.[7] The food-energy intake method consists of finding the consumption expenditure or income level at which food-energy intake is just enough to meet the requirements for good health and normal activity levels. Using expenditure and consumption surveys, the population is ordered in terms of income, and a group is identified as the first one for which the minimum nutritional requirements for a healthy life and normal activity

---

[7] In this simple exposition, we are expressing poverty line in per capita units under the assumption that the cost of meeting the basic needs is the same for each person in the household, regardless of the number of people in the household and their individual characteristics. The consideration of these issues gives rise to the discussion about scale equivalence and economies of scale, which is beyond the scope of our discussion.

are met.[8] The calorie consumption of households is calculated based on the food items purchased, and to incorporate the fact that caloric intakes vary for a certain level of income, the method generally calculates an expected value of intake, given the level of income. The average income or expenditure of the group of households selected as the reference group is considered the poverty line. This method does not imply the establishment of the basket of goods that allows the minimum nutritional requirements, nor the specification of the items included in nonfood consumption. Concerns about this method refer to the fact that the relationship between food-energy intake and income may change with differences in tastes, activity levels, relative prices, and publicly provided goods, among others (Ravallion, 2010). For example, the real income at which an urban household may attain a given caloric requirement can be higher than the corresponding one for a household in rural areas.

The cost of basic needs method consists of the establishment of an adequate consumption basket to cover certain basic needs, including food and nonfood items. The poverty line is established as the cost of the basic basket for each subgroup (generally regions) of the population; this implies selecting a group of households of a certain part of the income distribution (low income). In contrast to the food-energy intake method, instead of using the average expenditure of this group as the poverty line, the food they consume is chosen as a basic food basket. This basket of goods implies the incorporation of demand behavior for the satisfaction of nutritional requirements. There are infinite vectors of consumption that satisfy nutritional needs, but the method chooses the one that is consistent with the consumption decisions of a relevant reference group. As a second step, items corresponding to the nonfood expenditures of the reference group are added. These items include goods necessary to meet other basic needs, such as clothing, housing, transportation, and so on. This procedure gives rise to the Orshansky coefficient, which establishes the relationship between the basic food basket and the poverty line.[9]

Probably the most known poverty measure is the one proposed by the World Bank, based on a set of absolute poverty lines. Their objective is to measure poverty consistently across countries, reflecting similar levels of well-being in different countries. The original value of the World Bank poverty line was set at 1 dollar (PPP) per day by Ravallion, Datt, and Van de Walle (1991), using as

---

[8] The minimum caloric requirements for each household are set considering the characteristics of household members (age, sex, pregnancy, and breastfeeding).

[9] Milly Orshansky (1965) defined minimum food baskets for various types of households to calculate the first US poverty line. Given that the food share was about a third of total expenditure for households on the poverty line, this line was set as three times the value of the minimum food basket.

reference the poverty lines used in some of the world's poorest countries. It was then updated in 2022 to a value of US$2.15 per person per day, adjusted for purchasing power parity (2017 PPP). Since 2017, the World Bank publishes measurements based on two additional and higher lines, associated with the concepts of poverty in countries with higher incomes. The lines are $3.65 and $6.85 (2017 PPP) per person per day and were obtained as the median of the official lines for lower middle-income and upper middle-income countries, respectively, based on Jolliffe and Prydz (2016). In Latin America, the ECLAC calculated absolute poverty lines based on consumption baskets for the countries of the region during the 1990s, to be able to elaborate comparable overviews of poverty at the regional level. The methodology for the calculation of these poverty lines was recently updated (ECLAC, 2019).

The estimation of a SPL is based on the question *'What is the minimum monthly income amount that you estimate is necessary to meet the basic needs of your household?'*. It is important to notice that the approach is model based in the sense that a model is used to explain the interhousehold variation in the responses to survey questions; individual responses alone are not used to determine the poverty line directly. The respondent's answer to this MIQ will be denoted as Y_{min}. This minimum income depends on the actual household income and a series of other factors, including, for example, the household size. The formulation, following Goedhart et al. (1977) and Danziger et al. (1984), is as follows:

$$Y_{min} = f(Y, X), \tag{1}$$

where Y is the actual household income and X is a vector of other variables. The function f is monotonically increasing in Y, and there exists an income level Y^*_{min} defined by

$$Y^*_{min} = f\left(Y^*_{min}, X\right) \tag{2}$$

such that, for all incomes Y less than Y^*_{min}, it holds that $Y < Y_{min}$, and for all incomes Y greater than Y^*_{min}, it holds that $Y \geq Y_{min}$. Therefore, the income level Y^*_{min} is a candidate for the poverty line; people with income above this level tend to feel that their income is adequate, while those below that level tend to feel that it is not.

The approach was originally designed for use with panel data (Kapteyn et al., 1988), which allowed to test whether people gravitate toward some true minimum over time. It is expected that respondents who are above the true minimum would find that over time they have a better idea of what their true minimum is and would respond accordingly. For those below the true minimum, over time they would realize that they are underestimating their true income needs. However, most empirical applications of the SPL based on MIQ are based on cross-sectional data. The rationale behind choosing the intersection of the function $Y_{min} = f(Y, X)$ with the line $Y_{min} = Y$, represented by Y_{min}^*, is that only households for which income is equal to their minimally necessary income have realistic perceptions of this minimum income level (Kapteyn et al., 1988). Households with higher income are likely to overestimate their minimally necessary income, while those with lower income are expected to underestimate it (De Vos & Garner, 1991).

In line with Goedhart et al. (1977), Danziger et al. (1984), and De Vos & Garner (1991), a linear-logarithmic form is used to estimate equation (1). In addition to the logarithm of household income, other explanatory variables (x) are included. First, household size is an important factor in determining Y_{min}, as larger families will require a higher Y_{min}. Moreover, in the case of the United States, it has been observed that Y_{min} is lower for female-headed households (Danziger et al., 1984), while it increases with age, at a decreasing rate (De Vos & Garner, 1991). These authors also highlight the relationship between variables such as education, ethnic background, marital status of the household head, household composition, and the values of Y_{min} (Garner & De Vos, 1995; Garner & Short, 2003). Additionally, the area of residence is also a factor to consider since household needs can vary depending on the environment they are situated in (Colasanto et al., 1984; Garner & Short, 2003).

Based on the log-linear expression of equation (1), finding a subjective poverty threshold implies calculating the Y_{min}^* as the intersection of the relationship:

$$\ln(Y_{min}) = \alpha_0 + \alpha_1 \ln(y) + \alpha_2 x_2 + \alpha_3 x_3 + \dots + \alpha_n x_n + \epsilon. \tag{3}$$

Therefore, by equating for $Y_{min} = Y$ for different values of $x_2, \dots x_n$, the value of Y_{min}^*, the subjective poverty threshold, is defined as

$$Y^*(x_2 \dots x_n) = \exp\left(\frac{\widehat{\alpha}_0 + \widehat{\alpha}_2\, x_2 + \dots + \widehat{\alpha}_n x_n}{1 - \widehat{\alpha}_1}\right). \tag{4}$$

4 Previous Research about Subjective Poverty

Research on subjective poverty started over forty years ago with the pioneering study of Goedhart et al. (1977), who settled the ground of the MIQ methodology. After them, several studies applied this methodology with different specifications of the SPL. Most of the applications in this first stage were based on US data, with some notable exceptions as Van Praag et al. (1980) for several European countries. Later, some studies incorporated basic demographic determinants in the specification of the SPL, considering, for example, age, gender, and urban–rural location (Colasanto et al., 1984; Danziger et al., 1984). Further extensions included education, race, religion, disability, and marital status. An interesting strand of literature has underlined the role of previous family income and reference groups. Results indicate that households that have recently suffered a considerable decrease in their incomes report significantly higher minimum incomes than households with stable incomes (De Vos & Garner, 1991). Studies have also explored whether certain expenditures are considered when answering the MIQ question. Results indicate that housing and utility expenditures were considered when answering the question about minimum necessary income (De Vos & Garner, 1991; Garner & De Vos, 1995). Differences among European countries in terms of self-perception of poverty have been found to be related to different levels of household and community social capital endowments (Guagnano et al., 2016).

When subjective and objective poverty thresholds are compared, the former are higher (de Vos & Garner, 1991; Garner & Short, 2003). The divergence between the two poverty rates widens with household size, especially when objective poverty is measured based on per capita income. Larger households are more likely to be identified as income poor than to self-assess their status as poor. This may be explained by the lack of adjustment for lower per person costs of maintaining a given standard of living when individuals live together rather than apart. Equivalence scales implicit in subjective poverty measures tend to be greater than those usually considered in objective measures, posing interesting questions for methodological research (Ravallion & Lokshin, 2002).

Recent applications of subjective poverty are less focused on measurement and give more attention to the determinants of subjective poverty, also considering the discrepancies between subjective and objective poverty profiles. At the same time, the focus of the applications has shifted from the United States to developing countries. An interesting exception is Zelinsky et al. (2022), who estimate subjective poverty trends between 2004 and 2019 for 28 European countries based on the MIQ, as we do. They find poverty declines in more than half of the countries and argue that this reflects country trends that are not captured by official poverty indicators. In the case of Italy, Filandri et al. (2020) find that discrepancies between objective and subjective poverty are associated with the job stability of household members.

Several recent studies estimate subjective poverty for developing countries: Wang et al. (2020) for Rural China, and Maruejols et al. (2022) for China based on MIQ, Mahmood et al. (2019) for Pakistan and Posel & Rogan (2014) for South Africa based on a ten-step ladder of the relative position of the household in the distribution (steps 1 and 2 considered as poor), and Peng (2021) and Peng & Law (2023) for Hong Kong based on the self-perception of poverty.

The determinants of subjective poverty found in these studies are age and gender (male) of the household head and family size (reducing subjective poverty). Also, large and unusual expenditure on health and education tend to increase subjective poverty (Wang et al., 2020). The proportion of boys among children as well as residence in rural areas reduce subjective poverty, whereas unemployment, food insecurity, and physical insecurity increase it (Mahmood et al., 2019). Both studies identify a reduction in the probability of subjective poverty as per capita household income increases but differ in the effect of human capital and household wealth and assets. While Wang et al. (2020) observe that subjective poverty increases with human capital and household wealth and assets, Mahmood et al. (2019) observe a reduction in subjective poverty with education, household assets, and farmer's land. Mauejols et al. (2022) propose an explanation to these contrasting results: They find that subjective poverty is mostly associated with income for low-income households, but in the case of middle-income households, subjective poverty is associated with a combination of relatively low income, low endowments (land, consumption assets), and unusual large expenditure.

All the reviewed studies that compare subjective poverty against objective poverty find that the subjective poverty is significantly higher (Posel & Rogan, 2014; Wang et al., 2020; Peng, 2021; Zelinsky et al., 2022; Peng & Law, 2023). Mahmood et al. (2019) identify education, household size, own residence, and physical security among the factors that reduce objective poverty among households below the SPL. In the case of South Africa, Posel & Rogan (2014) conclude that subjective assessments of poverty are influenced by a range of factors in addition to the household's current economic resources, including the ability of the household to generate resources in the past and in the future, the household's access to basic services, and the average health status of household members. They also argue that these divergences are related to issues of economies of scale and adult equivalence, which deserve more attention. Alem et al. (2014) study the evolution of subjective and objective poverty for a 15-year span in urban Ethiopia and find that despite significant economic growth and a decrease in objective poverty, subjective poverty has largely stayed the same. They show that the household history in objective poverty is relevant to determining their perceptions, as households with a history of objective poverty continue to see themselves as poor, even when their material consumption improves. Conversely, employment protects against subjective poverty; households with any form of employment are less likely to perceive themselves as poor, even if they still experience objective poverty.

Some studies follow a slightly different strategy, focusing on the specific importance of one determinant of the subjective/objective poverty disagreement. One determinant that has gained increasing attention recently is the importance of social networks and reference groups as a subjective poverty determinant and as a possible explanation of the misalignment of subjective and objective poverty assessment. Peng (2021) studies for Hong Kong the importance of comparisons with parents and friends and finds that upward intergenerational mobility increases the probability of not feeling poor while being economically poor, and the opposite happens with downward mobility. In the case of friends, those who contrasted their social status with their lower-status friends were more likely to feel nonpoor, even if they were economically poor, and again the opposite relation is observed for those comparing to higher-status fiends. Overall, parents were a more important reference group than friends. Li & Cai (2024) explore how social networks affect subjective poverty through social support (emotional and instrumental) and reference groups in China. They find that larger and stronger social networks reduce subjective poverty. In addition, when the social network members serve as the reference group, the higher the status of individuals in the network, the weaker the subjective poverty. The effect of social networks as a reference group on subjective poverty depends on the objective poverty condition. Specifically, when individuals are objectively poor, the positive impact of social networks as a reference group on subjective poverty is diminished. The longitudinal study for urban Ethiopia (Alem et al. 2014) also finds that the relative economic position of households plays a major role in determining subjective poverty.

Another salient determinant of the discrepancy between objective and subjective poverty that has drawn recent attention is the expenditure pattern of households. Peng & Law (2023) and Peng (2023) study the importance of consumption patterns in explaining subjective poverty in Hong Kong. Peng & Law (2023) find that food-dominant consumption pattern increased the probability of feeling poor among the objectively poor as did the mortgage-high pattern among the economically nonpoor, both in reference to a balanced pattern. However, the significant association between the mortgage-high pattern and subjective poverty became insignificant after controlling for assets, indicating that this effect was most likely offset by the negative impacts of homeownership and assets. Peng (2023) focuses on the consumption of conspicuous goods (that display social status) and experiential goods (purchases made to acquire a life experience). He finds that spending on leisure, which encompasses both conspicuous and experiential consumption, raised the likelihood of feeling nonpoor among those who are objectively poor, and conversely decreased the likelihood of feeling poor among those who are economically nonpoor. These effects were influenced by self-perceived social status (via conspicuous consumption) but not by social connectedness (via experiential consumption).

In Latin America, studies about subjective poverty are scarce, and the existing ones are focused on one single country; no comparative studies for the region were identified. Many of them are not representative at the national level, as they are based on a specific city, region, or group of population. For Mexico, subjective poverty estimates are available for a specific region (Ortiz-Pech et al., 2019) and for five centers and southern states (Rojas & Jiménez, 2008), both based on self-perception. For Peru, estimates based on the MIQ are available by Monge & Winkerlried (2001) for extremely vulnerable households and Herrera (2002) for the total population. Colombian subjective poverty is estimated by Pinzón Gutiérrez (2017), Niño-Muñoz (2023), and Tobasura & Casas (2017). The first two studies are based on self-perception and the last one on Minimal Income Question, and only Pinzón Gutiérrez (2006) has national representativity. Estimates are also available for Argentina (Luchetti, 2006; based self-perception) and Uruguay (Scalese, 2022; based on the Minimal Income Question).

The studies that compare subjective and objective poverty in the region also find that subjective poverty is significantly higher (Monge & Winkerlried, 2001; Luchetti, 2006; Rojas & Jiménez, 2008; Tobasura & Casas, 2017; Scalese, 2022). Ortiz-Pech et al. (2019) find higher subjective poverty in a context where all the households are objectively poor, and Herrera (2002) finds that in Peru both types of poverty are similar.

As in the international context, the determinants of subjective poverty are studied for some countries in the region. Total household resources (income or expenditure) are identified as a factor reducing subjective poverty (Herrera, 2002; Pinzón Gutierrez, 2006; Rojas and Jiménez, 2008). Other factors positively associated with subjective poverty are undernutrition and violence (Pinzón Gutierrez, 2006). Household size, presence of children, parental education, married couples, and extended households are associated with lower subjective poverty (Herrera, 2002). Rojas & Jiménez (2008) also find that subjective poverty depends on the expectations regarding income and the comparison with reference groups. In her analysis at the municipal level of Colombia, Niño-Muñoz (2023) centers the attention on the study of the effects of institutions over the perception of poverty. Her results show that having a better rule of law and fiscal performance, reducing political fragmentation to have better governance, guaranteeing property rights, fostering the benefits of metropolitan areas, and improving citizen participation reduce the probability of feeling poor.

Last, two studies analyze the determinants of the discrepancy between subjective and objective poverty in the region. Luchetti (2006) observes that labor flexibility, qualification, and formality increase subjective well-being but not objective one in Argentina. For Uruguay, Scalese (2022) finds that the probability of discrepancies between absolute and subjective measures is affected by the characteristics of household members (unemployment, informality, education, and immigration), housing and household characteristics, and by the reception of public benefits (food baskets or cash transfers), as well as by the prevailing conditions of the reference group (defined by region of residence and age and education of household head).

5 Data and Methodological Aspects

The tradition of poverty measurement in Latin America is based on the consideration of absolute poverty lines, using the basic needs method. This tradition originated in the pioneering work of ECLAC at the end of the 1970s, which paved the way for the establishment of a common methodology for the region. At present, almost all the countries of the region have government bodies that carry out poverty measurements, using national absolute poverty lines (ECLAC, 2019). At the same time, ECLAC continues to calculate absolute poverty lines for Latin American countries to ensure comparability of poverty results across the region. Through this standardized methodology, based on the cost of basic needs method, ECLAC enables meaningful cross-country comparisons of poverty rates and trends in Latin America.[10]

The World Bank has also tracked global poverty since the early 1990s. Their key goal is to measure poverty consistently across countries, reflecting similar living standards. For Latin American countries, the World Bank threshold corresponds to $3.65 per person per day (PPP) in the cases of Bolivia, El Salvador, Guatemala, Honduras, Nicaragua, and Paraguay, which are classified as lower-middle-income countries. The corresponding WB threshold is $6.85 per person per day (PPP) in the cases of the upper-middle-income countries of the regions like Argentina, Brazil, Chile, Colombia, Costa Rica, Dominican Republic, Ecuador, Mexico, Panama, Peru, and Uruguay. The global extreme poverty line of $2.15 per person per day (PPP) applies to all countries, regardless of income level.

In this Element, we report results using national poverty lines to measure objective income poverty, which precludes direct cross-country comparisons. This methodological option is based on the fact that national poverty lines are typically developed with a deep understanding of local economic

---

[10] Details about the calculation of these poverty lines can be found in ECLAC (2019).

conditions, cultural norms, and societal expectations. These lines often better represent the social understanding and definition of poverty within each country and are policy relevant, as national governments refer to them to design and implement poverty reduction strategies and social programs. Moreover, these lines generally have greater acceptance and recognition among the country's inhabitants. However, to ensure the robustness of our findings, we also conduct parallel analyses using the ECLAC and World Bank poverty lines, recognizing its value as a standardized measure for cross-country comparisons.

This study is based on surveys that include questions regarding subjective poverty. In the cases of Brazil (2017–2018), Colombia (2016–2017), El Salvador (2005–2006), Paraguay (2011–2012), and Uruguay (2016–2017), expenditure and income surveys are used. For Ecuador (2013–2014) we use the life conditions survey, and for Peru (2018) we use the National Household Survey. Table 1 summarizes the main characteristics of the surveys mentioned here.

Table 1 Characteristics of surveys

Country	Survey	Year	Coverage	# households
Brazil	Household Budget Survey	2017–2018	National	65,800
Colombia	National Household Budget Survey	2016–2017	National	86,222
Ecuador	Life Conditions Survey	2013–2014	National	28,970
El Salvador	National Survey of Household Income and Expenditure	2005–2006	National	4,381
Paraguay	Survey of Income and Expenses and Living Conditions	2011–2012	National	5,288
Peru	National Household Survey	2018	National	33,900
Uruguay	National Survey of Household Income and Expenditure	2016–2017	National	6,880

Source: Author's ellaboration.

Although all the countries in our analysis are classified as middle income, significant differences emerge in their social contexts, reflecting the diverse socioeconomic landscapes within this broad category. Table A.1 summarizes various social and labor market indicators for the seven countries, revealing a consistent grouping pattern that underscores the heterogeneity of middle-income nations. At one end of the spectrum, El Salvador stands out as the most disadvantaged country in our analysis, with the highest poverty rates (exceeding 50 percent), lowest female labor participation (43 percent), and lowest Human Development Index (0.64). These figures paint a stark picture of the challenges faced by El Salvador in terms of economic development, gender equality, and overall quality of life for its citizens. The high poverty rate, in particular, suggests deep-rooted structural issues. In contrast, Uruguay emerges as the most advantaged country across almost all indicators, boasting a poverty rate of 4 percent, female labor participation of 58 percent, and a Human Development Index of 0.81. Peru follows closely, with a poverty rate of 17 percent, female participation of 64 percent, and a Human Development Index of 0.77, indicating substantial progress in social development and gender equality in the labor market. The remaining countries occupy an intermediate position, characterized by poverty rates ranging from 21 percent to 31 percent, female labor participation between 54 percent and 59 percent, and Human Development Index scores between 0.71 and 0.76. This middle group demonstrates the complexity of development trajectories as these nations have made significant strides in some areas while still facing considerable challenges in others. Notably, these countries also exhibit the highest inequality within our sample, as measured by the Gini coefficient. This suggests that while these nations have achieved a certain level of overall development, the benefits of this progress may not be evenly distributed among their populations.

The absolute poverty lines we are considering are constructed by the National Statistical Offices in each country, following the cost of basic needs method, except for Brazil. As Brazil does not have an official poverty line, we follow the usual practice in the literature and consider half minimum wage as the poverty line. Details about the absolute poverty thresholds and their calculation in each country are presented in Table 2. As explained, our choice of the national poverty lines as the basis of our analysis is derived from the consideration that these lines express more accurately the social sense of poverty than other poverty thresholds. Despite this, and as a robustness check for our results, we also perform the calculations using ECLAC's poverty lines, and report the main results in the Appendix.

To elaborate the SPL, we follow the method discussed in Section 2. In our case, the control variables considered for the estimation include household

Table 2 Objective absolute poverty lines for selected Latin American countries

Country	Poverty line construction
Brazil	Brazil does not have an official poverty methodology. To construct a per capita poverty line, half the value of the minimum wage is usually taken as a reference.
Colombia	The poverty line is the minimum per capita cost of a basic basket of goods (food and nonfood) in each geographic area, based on the 2016–2017 National Household Budget Survey.
Ecuador	The fifth round of the Quality-of-Life Survey (ECV) conducted in 2006 was used to draw both the official extreme poverty line, which reflects a minimum threshold of 2,144 Kcal per person per day, and the official moderate poverty line, which uses an Engel coefficient of 56 percent. The poverty lines are updated across time using the total CPI.
El Salvador	The country uses the Cost of Basic Needs method for the poverty estimates, providing two estimates: (i) extreme poverty (the cost of a basic consumption basket that would allow household members to consume a minimal amount of calories) and (ii) moderate poverty (the cost of an extended consumption basket, equal to twice the value of the basic consumption basket). The official line used by El Salvador was constructed in 1982 and was based on food spending patterns from the 1976 Family Budget Survey.
Paraguay	The extreme poverty line corresponds to the monetary value of the basic food basket, which reflects minimums thresholds of 2117 and 2291 Kcal for urban and rural regions. The value of the total poverty line is equal to the value of the extreme poverty line multiplied by the Engel coefficient, which is 38 percent for urban regions and 48.8 percent for rural areas. The structure of the basic food basket and the basic consumption basket was updated following the 2011–2012 Income and Expenditure and Living Conditions Survey.
Peru	Peru uses monetary poverty lines to measure extreme and total poverty with per capita consumption as the welfare measure. The total poverty line represents the minimum cost of acquiring a basket of goods and services necessary to achieve adequate living conditions, and this basket varies by geographic region as well as by rural and urban areas. It was constructed based on the 2010 National Household Expenditure Survey.

Table 2 (cont.)

Country	Poverty line construction
Uruguay	The poverty line corresponds to the updated monetary value of the basic food and nonfood baskets considering economies of scale for the nonfood expenditures introduced by geographical area. The poverty line is constructed based on Household Consumption and Income Survey of 2005–2006.

Source: Author's elaboration.

income, number of members of the household, age of the head of household and its square, binary variables identifying female household head, non-white household head and urban households, marital status of household head, household type, and years of education of the household head (see Table A.2).

Once we classify households in terms of objective and subjective poverty, we evaluate the correlation and overlapping of both measures. With this objective, we calculate the Cramer V correlation between both types of measure and redundancy coefficients, following Santos & Villatoro (2018).

Given two poverty measures, j and j', the Cramer's V coefficient is calculated as

$$Cramer's\,V = \frac{\left(p_{00}^{jj'} * p_{11}^{jj'}\right) - \left(p_{10}^{jj'} * p_{01}^{jj'}\right)}{\left[p_{+1}^{j'} * p_{1+}^{j} * p_{+0}^{j'} * p_{0+}^{j}\right]^{1/2}}, \tag{5}$$

where $p_{00}^{jj'}$ is the proportion of people nonpoor in both j and j', $p_{11}^{jj'}$ is the proportion of people poor in both j and j', $p_{10}^{jj'}$ is the proportion of people poor in j but not in j', and $p_{01}^{jj'}$ is the proportion of people poor in j' but not in j. $p_{+1}^{j'}$ and p_{1+}^{j} are the proportions of people poor in j' and j, respectively, whereas $p_{+0}^{j'}$ and p_{0+}^{j} are the proportions of people nonpoor in j' and j, respectively. In other words, the Cramer's V is defined as the product of matches minus product of mismatches adjusting for the marginal distribution of the variables.

The redundancy measure R^0 is a more precise indicator showing the matches between deprivations in both measures as a proportion of the minimum of the two poverty measures.

$$R^0 = p_{11}^{jj'} / min\left(p_{+1}^{j'}, p_{+1}^{j}\right), 0 \le R^0 \le 1. \tag{6}$$

Finally, to analyze the concordance between households classified as poor under the subjective and objective approaches, we use a probit model. This allows us to identify the factors associated with the lack of agreement between these measures. As discussed in Section 6.3, our results indicate that the largest discrepancies occur among households that are not poor in objective terms but consider themselves as poor, that is, they are subjectively poor. For this reason, our probit model takes the set of households that are not poor in absolute terms and investigates the factors associated with their perception of themselves as poor.

6 Subjective and Objective Poverty

We present our main results in three subsections: first the estimations of the SPL and the comparison with the objective poverty lines in Latin America, second the comparison of poverty prevalence, last the results for the subjective poverty and the superposition with national poverty lines.

6.1 Subjective and Objective Poverty Thresholds in Latin America

Our SPLs are estimated based on models with control variables, presented in Table A.2. The results of the models are as expected in the seven countries; the minimum household income is positively related to the perceived household income and with the number of household members. The other control variables also show the expected behavior. In general terms, the minimum income is positively related with the age of the household head (in decreasing terms) and with their education, and negatively related to female and non-white household heads. The result that households with reference persons with less education report needing less than those with higher education has been interpreted as a reference group effects (Garner & Short, 2003). Also, households with a married or cohabiting head are associated with higher minimum income answers than singles, while the evidence for separated, divorced, and widows or widowers is not conclusive across countries. All the household types are associated with higher minimum income than unipersonal households, especially couples with children and extended households (with relatives). These results go in the same line as De Vos & Garner (1991) (age), Garner & de Vos (1995) and Garner & Short (2003) (education), and Danzinger et al. (1984) (female household head).

Using the coefficients derived from the previous estimation, the SPL is constructed by substituting them in equation (4). Thus, we obtain a different value of the line for each household depending on its characteristics. In Figure 1, we compare the SPL by veintiles of per capita income of the country with the minimum income (MIQ) declared by the households. Both variables are expressed in PPP dollars of 2015.

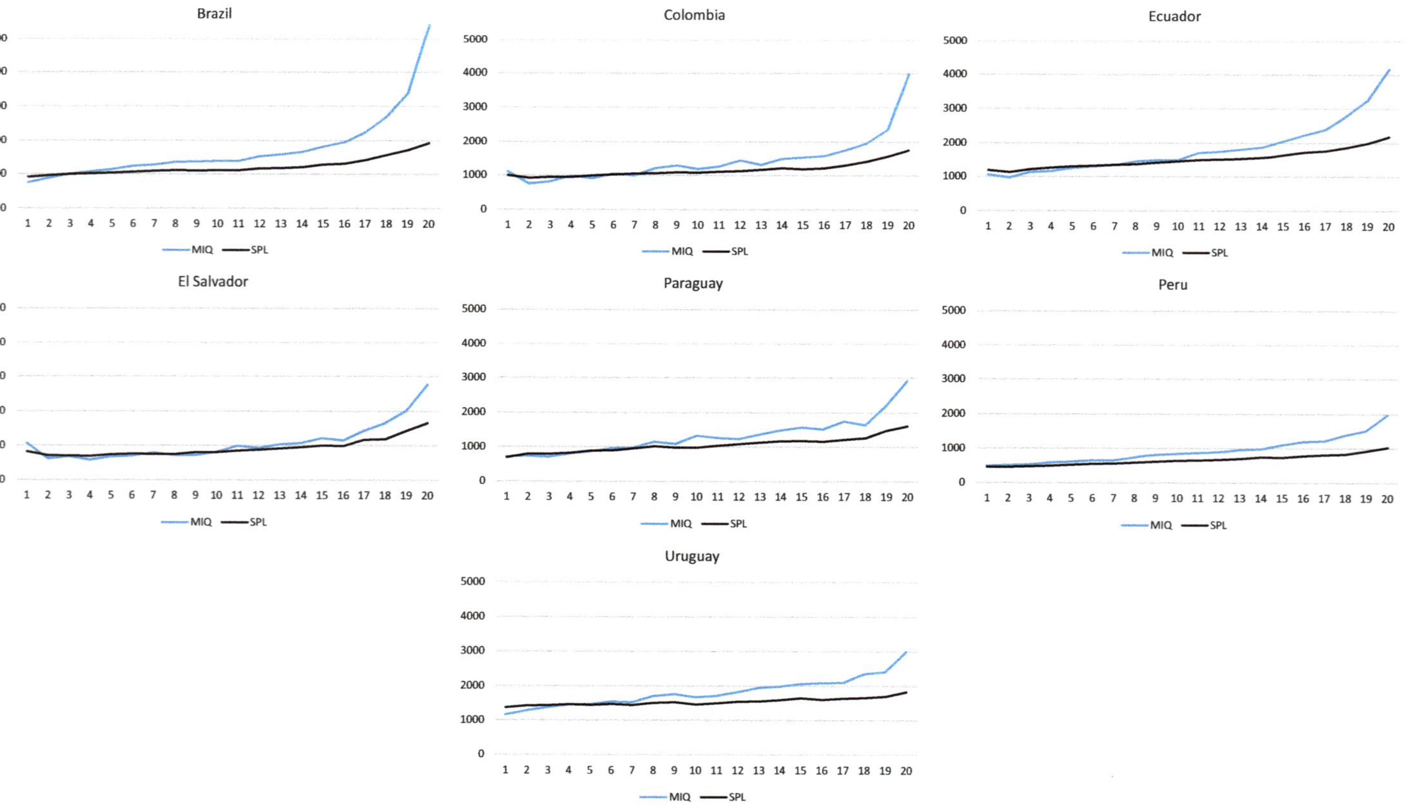

Figure 1 Minimum income question (MIQ) and subjective poverty line (SPL) by per capita household income.

Notes: Minimum income question and SPL expressed in 2015 PPP dollars. Per capita household income in ventiles.

Source: Based on household surveys from Brazil (2017–2018), Colombia (2016–2017), Ecuador (2014), El Salvador (2005–2006), Paraguay (2011–2012), Peru (2018), and Uruguay (2016–2017).

The minimum income increases with household per capita income in all the considered countries, which is consistent with Goedhart et al. (1977) and Danziger et al. (1984). In all the countries, households with income over the median (ventile 10 and over) tend to overestimate the minimum necessary income as it is higher than the SPL, even after adjusting for all the included controls. Overestimation increases with income and is particularly high for households of the higher deciles. The behavior in the lower half of the distribution is not consistent across countries. In general terms, poorer households declare a minimum income that is close to or slightly under the SPL.

The comparison between the objective and SPLs reveals systematic differences. As shown in Table 3, the average SPL is almost always higher than the objective poverty line, as reported in almost all the previous research. The difference is higher when ECLAC or World Bank thresholds are considered, given that those poverty lines are lower than national poverty lines, except for Ecuador. The range of variation of the absolute poverty lines between countries is much smaller than that of SPLs. The average SPL is between 8 percent and 167 percent higher than the national objective poverty line, depending on the country, with these extremes corresponding to Paraguay and Ecuador. Only in Peru both thresholds are virtually equal, consistent with previous results for the country (Herrera, 2002).

The SPLs are on average 60 percent higher than the objective national (absolute) ones. This is consistent with the results found for the European Union, in which the average difference between the subjective and official lines is 50 percent (Zelinsky et al., 2022). Figure 2 summarizes the ratios between the subjective and objective poverty lines found in the literature using the MIQ, including our results. As in the European case, there is a large variation in our data, with the ratios of subjective to official poverty ranging from 1.00 (Peru) to 2.67 (Ecuador).[11] Results for rural China also reflect higher subjective than official poverty lines, with a ratio closer to the maximum of our range (Wang et al. 2020). In any case, our results are in line with the range found in previous studies.

6.2 Subjective and Objective Poverty Prevalence in Latin America

After we estimate the SPL for each household, we calculate the poverty prevalence. All those households for which income is below the corresponding subjective line will be considered subjectively poor, while those households with income above the subjective line will be considered nonpoor in subjective

---

[11] The range for Europe is 0.75 (Finland and the UK) to over 3 (Greece, Romania, and Bulgaria) (Zelinsky et al., 2022).

Table 3 Subjective and objective absolute poverty lines. Average values (2015 PPP dollars)

	Objective – Absolute			Subjective	Percent difference (Sub.-Obj.)		
	National	**ECLAC**	**WB**		**National**	**ECLAC**	**WB**
Brazil	624	517	496	1211	94%	134%	144%
Colombia	726	654	553	1157	59%	77%	109%
Ecuador	565	657	606	1510	167%	130%	149%
El Salvador	858	859	400	926	8%	8%	131%
Paraguay	843	690	374	1056	25%	53%	182%
Peru	661	585	621	660	0%	13%	6%
Uruguay	918	582	465	1539	68%	165%	231%

Source: Absolute poverty lines are taken from official indicators for each country, ECLAC, and the World Bank. Subjective poverty lines are own estimations based on household expenditure surveys from Brazil (2017–2018), Colombia (2016–2017), Ecuador (2014), El Salvador (2005–2006), Paraguay (2011–2012), Peru (2018), and Uruguay (2016–2017).

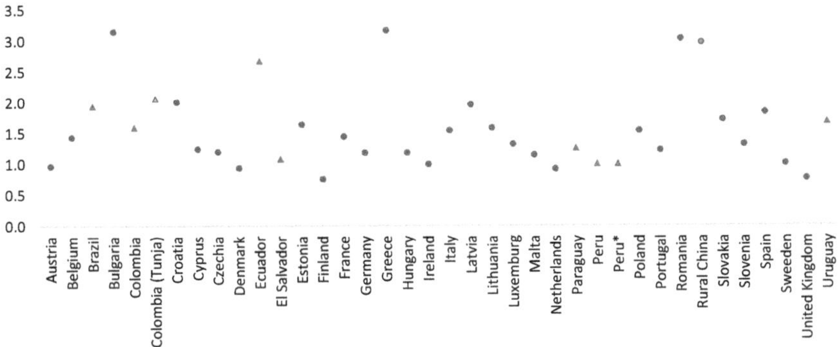

Figure 2 Ratio between subjective and objective poverty lines.

Notes: Ratios of European countries based on Zelinsky et al. (2022), for one-adult households, in dark gray circles. Rural China based on Wang et al. (2020), in light gray circle. Latin American data in triangles, own estimations in red. Peru* is based on Herrera (2002), original results presented by region, in the figure we present the regional mean. Colombia (Tunja) based on Tobasura and Casas (2017) for the Tunja city of Colombia.

terms. For objective poverty, we consider a household as poor if its income is under the official national poverty line, or the ECLAC or World Bank threshold. Note that poverty incidence may be different from the official figures as official poverty measures are calculated based on household surveys, while we are considering expenditure surveys.

The results depicted in Figure 3 indicate that the lowest levels of subjective poverty are reported in Peru, Brazil, and Uruguay, with figures between 28 percent and 33 percent, and the highest in El Salvador and Colombia, with over 60 percent of the population considered as subjective poor. These figures are not entirely comparable as the reference years of the surveys differ substantially in a period of important reductions in poverty in the region. While the results from El Salvador are from 2005–2006, the figures from Brazil, Colombia, Peru, and Uruguay refer to 2016–2018.

The ranking of countries is similar to the one that arises considering objective poverty with national, ECLAC, or World Bank thresholds, except for Peru and Ecuador. In the case of Peru, this comes from the very small difference between both indicators, which locates the country in the low range of subjective poverty, but in medium range of objective poverty. In Ecuador, the re-ranking comes from the opposite situation, as the gap between both measures is the highest. Thus, the country has one of the lowest objective poverty rates of the region but one of the highest subjective poverty rates.

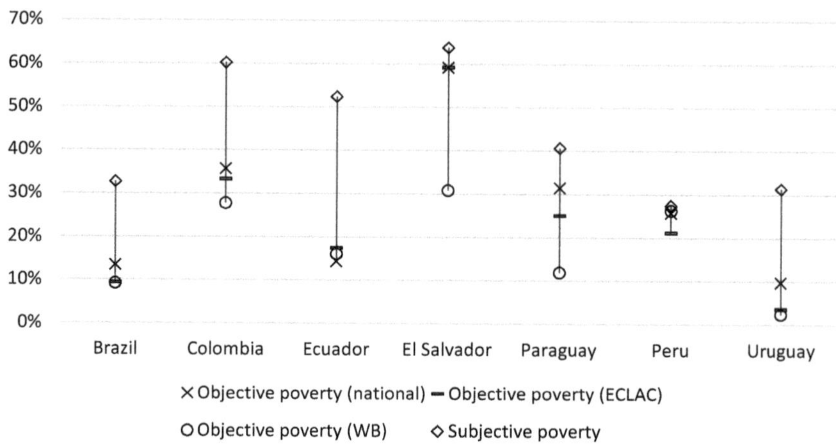

Figure 3 Subjective and objective household poverty.

Source: Based on household surveys from Brazil (2017–2018), Colombia (2016–2017), Ecuador (2014), El Salvador (2005–2006), Paraguay (2011–2012), Peru (2018), and Uruguay (2016–2017).

The gaps between the prevalence of subjective and objective poverty range from two points in Peru to thirty-eight points in Ecuador. When ECLAC or World Bank poverty lines are considered, the gaps tend to be some points higher. The exception is Ecuador, where ECLAC poverty line is lower than the national poverty line, but the difference in the incidence of objective poverty under these two thresholds is of small magnitude. We observe three different situations in terms of this gap: Peru, Paraguay, and El Salvador with small differences between subjective and objective poverty (under ten points); Brazil, Colombia, and Uruguay with gaps around twenty points; and Ecuador with a difference of thirty-eight points.

This regularity replicates within countries. As shown in Table A.3, subjective poverty is higher in almost all cases (rural and urban households, white and non-white household heads). Rural and non-white headed households show lower differences between subjective and objective poverty, while suffering from higher poverty rates, both subjective and objective. This can be explained by two different hypotheses. First, poorer households evaluate their situation more accurately in comparison with less poor households. Second, in areas/groups where overall poverty is higher, it is easier for a household to identify as poor.

These results are different from those found for European countries, in which SPLs are higher for urban than rural areas (Zelinsky et al., 2022). Similarly, Mahmood et al. (2018) also identify higher subjective poverty in urban contexts for Pakistan, while objective poverty is higher in rural areas. Several studies show that the relationship between subjective well-being and geography is not consistent and can depend on differences in price levels, expectations on minimum income, and differences in labor market opportunities, among others (Dolan et al., 2008; Shucksmith et al., 2009; Jansky & Kolcunova, 2017).

To further investigate the characteristics of the subjective poor and objective poor, Table 4 presents a comprehensive comparison of demographic and socio-economic characteristics between both populations, considering national objective lines. This detailed analysis reveals several important patterns and distinctions between these two groups across the countries studied.

For all countries in our study, subjectively poor households are consistently smaller and have fewer children compared to objectively poor households. This finding aligns with previous studies and suggests that perceptions of poverty may be influenced by household size and composition differently than objective measures. It's possible that larger households with more children feel better equipped to manage their resources despite having lower per capita incomes.

Interestingly, characteristics typically associated with worse material conditions, such as female-headed households, immigrant status, and non-white household heads, are more prevalent among the objectively poor than among those who identify themselves as poor. This pattern holds across most countries, although the differences are not always statistically significant. This discrepancy could indicate that these groups may have developed coping mechanisms or have different reference points for assessing their economic well-being.

Another consistent finding across all countries is that rural households represent a higher share among the objectively poor than among the subjectively poor. This rural–urban divide in poverty perception versus objective measurement could reflect differences in cost of living, access to services, or cultural factors that influence how rural residents perceive their economic status.

Employment rates tend to be lower among objectively poor households, which is an expected finding given the strong link between employment and income. However, it's worth noting that this difference is not statistically significant in some countries, suggesting that employment alone may not always be a clear differentiator between subjective and objective poverty.

The educational level of household heads presents an intriguing pattern. In most countries, subjectively poor households have higher levels of education compared to objectively poor households. This finding is particularly interesting as it suggests that higher education might lead to increased awareness of one's relative economic position or higher aspirations, resulting in a greater likelihood of perceiving oneself as poor even when above the objective poverty

Table 4 Sociodemographic characteristics of objective and subjective poor

	Brazil			Colombia			Ecuador			El Salvador			Paraguay			Peru			Uruguay		
	Obj. poor	Subj. poor		Obj. poor	Subj. poor		Obj. poor	Subj. poor		Obj. poor	Subj. poor		Obj. poor	Subj. poor		Obj. poor	Subj. poor		Obj. poor	Subj. poor	
Hosehold size	4.2	2.9	*	3.9	3.1	*	4.2	3.3	*	4.6	4.0	*	4.5	3.5	*	4.4	2.8	*	3.7	2.4	*
Number of children (under 12 years old)	1.2	0.6	*	1.0	0.7	*	1.4	0.9	*	1.3	1.1	*	1.5	1.0	*	1.1	0.5	*	0.9	0.3	*
Number of adults (above 65 years old)	0.1	0.2	*	0.3	0.3	*	0.3	0.3	*	0.3	0.3		0.3	0.3		0.6	0.5	*	0.2	0.4	*
% of employed (25–59 years old)	57.1%	63.5%	*	60.6%	65.8%	*	72.0%	74.9%	*	69.8%	70.0%		77.0%	78.1%		73.3%	74.5%		63.8%	70.2%	*
% of urban households	69.8%	84.2%	*	86.1%	88.9%	*	42.1%	65.4%	*	52.4%	59.2%	*	46.7%	55.0%	*	53.7%	62.9%	*	92.5%	83.3%	*
% of households headed by women	46.2%	46.6%		41.3%	39.2%	*	32.1%	29.2%	*	33.6%	33.7%		37.9%	37.1%		27.7%	33.4%	*	61.3%	49.9%	*
% of households headed by a white person	23.3%	35.6%	*	87.3%	88.9%	*	2.8%	3.8%	*				34.6%	50.4%	*	4.4%	3.9%		85.1%	91.0%	*

% of households headed by an inmigrant						0.7%	1.0%		0.6%	0.7%	1.3%	2.5%	*				2.2%	3.0%			
% of women (>18 years old)	53.6%	54.0%	54.3%	52.9%	*	56.5%	53.5%	*	55.6%	55.4%	52.9%	52.9%		48.5%	50.7%	*	54.0%	53.8%			
Maximum years of education of household	9.8	10.0	9.7	10.2	*	8.0	9.4	*	7.7	8.1	8.2	8.9	*	8.6	9.0	*	9.2	9.4			

Notes: * Indicates that the means are statically different at a 95 percent confidence interval. Objective poverty is measured considering official national poverty lines.

Source: Based on household surveys from Brazil (2017–2018), Colombia (2016–2017), Ecuador (2014), El Salvador (2005–2006), Paraguay (2011–2012), Peru (2018), and Uruguay (2016–2017).

line. However, it's important to note that in Brazil and Uruguay, these differences in education levels are not statistically significant, indicating that this pattern may not be universal across all contexts.

These observed differences between subjectively and objectively poor populations have important implications for our understanding of poverty and for policy design. They suggest that objective measures of poverty, while crucial, may not fully capture the lived experience of economic hardship as perceived by individuals and households. The higher prevalence of certain vulnerable groups (female-headed households, immigrants, non-white individuals) among the objectively poor, despite not necessarily identifying as poor, could indicate a need for targeted interventions that address not only income levels but also other factors contributing to economic vulnerability.

The rural–urban divide in subjective versus objective poverty highlights the importance of considering geographic factors in poverty alleviation strategies. Policies may need to be tailored differently for rural and urban areas, taking into account not just income levels but also perceptions of economic well-being. The relationship between education and subjective poverty, where present, raises questions about the role of education in shaping economic expectations and perceptions. It suggests that poverty-reduction strategies should consider not only improving educational attainment but also addressing the potential mismatch between educational achievement and economic opportunities.

These findings underscore the complexity of poverty as both an objective condition and a subjective experience. They point to the value of incorporating both objective and subjective measures in poverty assessments to gain a more comprehensive understanding of economic well-being. The differences observed between these two groups of poor populations signal the need for multifaceted approaches to poverty reduction that address both material deprivation and perceived economic hardship.

In the following section, we provide a deeper exploration into these patterns, exploring potential explanations for the divergences between subjective and objective poverty and discussing their implications for policy and future research. This analysis will contribute to a more nuanced understanding of poverty in Latin America and inform more targeted and effective poverty alleviation strategies.

6.3 The Overlap between Subjective and Objective Poverty

We further explore the overlap between objective and subjective poverty in Table 5 and Figure 4, considering national poverty lines for the measurement of

Table 5 Subjective and objective poverty overlap

			Objective poverty		
			Poor	**Nonpoor**	*Total*
Brazil	Subjective	Poor	12%	21%	*33%*
	poverty	Nonpoor	1%	66%	*67%*
		Total	*13%*	*87%*	*100%*
Colombia	Subjective	Poor	33%	27%	*60%*
	poverty	Nonpoor	2%	37%	*40%*
		Total	*36%*	*64%*	*100%*
Ecuador	Subjective	Poor	14%	38%	*52%*
	poverty	Nonpoor	0%	47%	*48%*
		Total	*14%*	*86%*	*100%*
El Salvador	Subjective	Poor	52%	12%	*64%*
	poverty	Nonpoor	7%	29%	*36%*
		Total	*59%*	*41%*	*100%*
Paraguay	Subjective	Poor	27%	14%	*41%*
	poverty	Nonpoor	5%	55%	*59%*
		Total	*31%*	*69%*	*100%*
Peru	Subjective	Poor	16%	11%	*28%*
	poverty	Nonpoor	10%	63%	*72%*
		Total	*26%*	*74%*	*100%*
Uruguay	Subjective	Poor	8%	23%	*31%*
	poverty	Nonpoor	1%	67%	*69%*
		Total	*10%*	*90%*	*100%*

Notes: Objective poverty is measured considering official national poverty lines.
Source: Based on household surveys from Brazil (2017–2018), Colombia (2016–2017), Ecuador (2014), El Salvador (2005–2006), Paraguay (2011–2012), Peru (2018), and Uruguay (2016–2017).

objective poverty.[12] A key observation is that subjective poverty is consistently larger than objective poverty across all countries. This pattern results in two predominant categories of poor individuals: those who are poor by both measures and those who are only subjectively poor. This finding underscores the importance of considering subjective measures alongside objective ones to gain a more comprehensive understanding of perceived economic hardship.

The most significant discrepancy between the two classifications of poverty arises from a substantial proportion of the population being considered nonpoor

---

[12] Results corresponding to ECLAC and World Bank poverty lines are similar; they are available upon request to the authors.

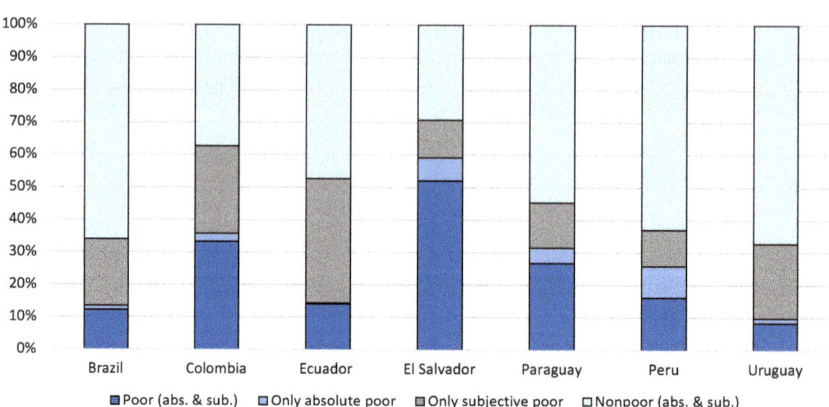

Figure 4 Subjective and objective poverty overlap.

Notes: Objective poverty is measured considering official national poverty lines.
Source: Based on household surveys from Brazil (2017–2018), Colombia (2016–2017), Ecuador (2014), El Salvador (2005–2006), Paraguay (2011–2012), Peru (2018), and Uruguay (2016–2017).

under the objective poverty line but poor according to subjective criteria. This discrepancy varies considerably across countries. In Brazil, 21 percent of the population falls into this category, while in Colombia, it rises to 27 percent. Ecuador shows the highest discrepancy, with 38 percent of its population considering themselves poor despite being above the objective poverty line. El Salvador and Peru have lower rates at 12 percent and 11 percent, respectively, while Paraguay stands at 14 percent. Uruguay, despite its relatively high economic development in the region, still sees 23 percent of its population in this category. These figures highlight the substantial proportion of people who, despite having incomes above the objective poverty line, perceive themselves as poor. This discrepancy is particularly pronounced in Ecuador, where it affects more than a third of the population.

Conversely, the proportion of individuals classified as poor under the objective threshold but not considering themselves poor is generally smaller, involving less than 5 percent of the population in most countries. The exceptions are El Salvador and Peru, where this discrepancy accounts for 7 percent and 10 percent of the population, respectively. In El Salvador, this can be attributed to the high overall prevalence of poverty, while in Peru, it relates to the small difference between the subjective and objective poverty lines.

Figure 4 provides a visual representation of these overlaps and discrepancies. The stacked bar chart clearly illustrates the varying compositions of poverty across the seven countries. The sections represent those who are poor by both measures, those who are only subjectively poor, those who are only objectively poor, and those who are nonpoor by both measures. This visual representation allows for easy comparison across countries and highlights the varying degrees of alignment between subjective and objective poverty measures.

Based on the patterns observed in Figure 4 and Table 5, we can identify three distinct groups of countries. The first group, characterized by low poverty, includes Brazil, Peru, and Uruguay. In these countries, over 60 percent of households are not poor by either measure. Among those considered poor, the majority are only subjectively poor in Brazil and Uruguay (59 percent and 70 percent of the poor, respectively), while in Peru, about one-third fall into this category. This suggests that in these relatively more developed economies, perceptions of poverty may be influenced by factors beyond absolute income levels.

The second group, comprising Ecuador and Paraguay, shows medium levels of poverty, with approximately half of the population not poor under either measure. However, the composition of poverty differs significantly between them. In Ecuador, 73 percent of the poor are only subjectively poor, indicating a large discrepancy between objective and subjective measures. In contrast, in Paraguay, only 30 percent of the poor are subjectively poor, with the majority (59 percent) being poor by both measures. This stark difference highlights the importance of country-specific factors in shaping poverty perceptions.

The third group, consisting of Colombia and El Salvador, exhibits high levels of poverty, with less than 40 percent of the population nonpoor by both measures. Again, there are notable differences between the two countries. In El Salvador, 74 percent of the poor (or 52 percent of the total population) are poor by both measures, indicating a high alignment between subjective and objective poverty. In Colombia, both types of poverty combined represent 53 percent of the poor, suggesting a more complex interplay between objective conditions and subjective perceptions.

These groupings reveal the heterogeneity in poverty patterns across Latin America. That substantial proportion of individuals who are subjectively poor but not objectively poor in many countries raises important questions about the factors influencing perceptions of poverty. These may include relative deprivation, economic insecurity, or unmet expectations based on education or social comparisons. Understanding these factors is crucial for developing more comprehensive and effective poverty alleviation strategies.

The overlap structure is similar between rural and urban areas, although the prevalence of subjective and objective poverty differs (see Table A.3). The only exception is Colombia, where the most prevalent situation in rural households is to be poor by both measures, while in urban households, as in the total population, the most prevalent situation is to be identified as nonpoor by both measures. In the second most important category we find discrepancies between regions in three countries.

Subjective and objective poverty are related to household per capita income. In the case of objective poverty, this relation is straightforward, as poverty arises from the comparison of per capita income with a poverty line. Subjective poverty is also related to income, as seen in the previous section, at least at the individual level.[13] Figure 5 plots subjective and objective poverty by household per capita income ventiles. As expected, average objective poverty is 100 percent for the poorer ventiles, drops sharply around the ventil that corresponds to the national poverty line, and is then zero for the richer ventiles. The exceptions to this shape correspond to countries in which the official poverty line changes by some characteristics of the household (i.e. region in Colombia, number of members in Uruguay). In these countries, the relationship between poverty and per capita income can be nonlinear.

Subjective poverty depicts a more continuous shape, always downward sloped. Subjective poverty is relevant in almost all the per capita income distribution: average subjective poverty is under 10 percent for the richer 30 percent of the population in Brazil, the top 25 percent in Peru and Uruguay, 15 percent in Paraguay, and only in the last decile for Colombia, Ecuador, and El Salvador.

Furthermore, the population that considers itself poor in subjective terms but is not poor according to the objective measurement of poverty is generally located from the first quartile of the income distribution onward. This discrepancy between subjective and objective poverty measures highlights the complex nature of economic well-being and the limitations of relying solely on income-based metrics to assess poverty. In fact, between 65 percent and 70 percent of this population concentrates in the second and third quintiles in Brazil, Ecuador, Paraguay, and Peru, whereas the figure is close to 60 percent in Colombia and Uruguay (see Table A.4). This concentration in the middle quintiles of the income distribution is particularly noteworthy, as it suggests that a significant portion of the population that feels economically disadvantaged actually falls within what might be considered the "middle class" based on objective measures. This phenomenon underscores the importance of considering subjective perceptions of poverty alongside objective indicators when formulating social and economic policies.

---

[13] As previously mentioned, the Easterlin Paradox states that income is positively correlated with subjective well-being at the individual level, but this relation disappears at the aggregate level, which could be partially explained by inequality (Oishi & Kesebir, 2015).

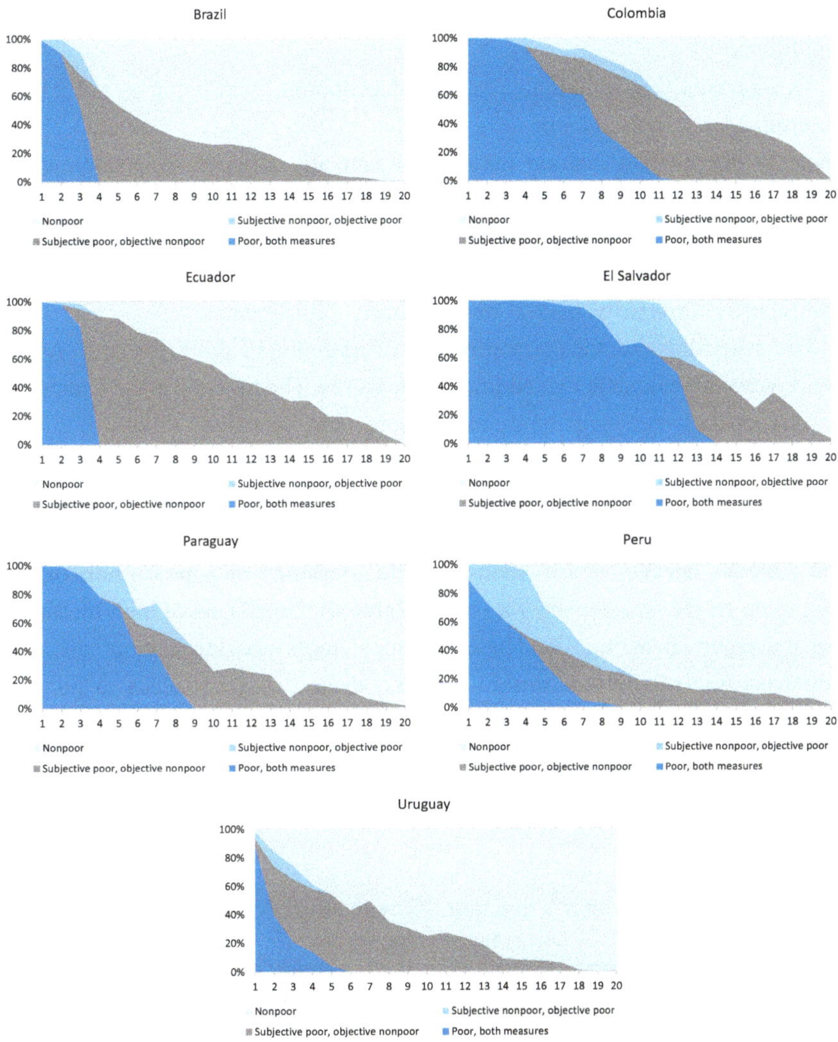

Figure 5 Subjective and objective poverty by per capita household income.

Notes: Per capita household income in ventiles. Objective poverty is measured considering official national poverty lines.

Source: Based on household surveys from Brazil (2017–2018), Colombia (2016–2017), Ecuador (2014), El Salvador (2005–2006), Paraguay (2011–2012), Peru (2018), and Uruguay (2016–2017).

The exception is El Salvador, where this population tends to locate to the right of the median distribution. This unique pattern in El Salvador reflects distinct economic conditions and probably social expectations that may influence perceptions of poverty. As discussed in Section 2, El Salvador stands out within this group of countries as the one with most disadvantaged economic conditions.

This reveals that individuals' sense of economic well-being is not solely determined by their income level relative to the poverty threshold. Those close to the median income may feel financially strained or economically insecure despite meeting official poverty thresholds, indicating that objective measures of poverty may not fully capture the lived experiences of economic hardship. Subjective poverty seems to reflect the nature of economic hardship and financial insecurity, instead of basic needs fulfillment.

To further illustrate the correlation and overlapping of subjective and objective poverty we calculate two additional measures. The first one is the Cramer V correlation between both types of measure (see Santos & Villatoro, 2018), which is defined as the product of matches minus product of mismatches adjusting for the marginal distribution of the variables. The other measure is the redundancy measure R^0 proposed by Alkire and Ballon (2012), which shows the matches between deprivations in both measures as a proportion of the minimum of the two poverty measures (Table 6). Details about both measures are presented in Section 4. These statistical tools provide a more nuanced understanding of the relationship between these two approaches to poverty measurement, offering insights into both their alignment and divergence across different contexts. As expected, the correlation between both measures is relatively high, ranging from 0.42 in Ecuador to 0.61 in Paraguay and El

Table 6 Cramer's V and redundacy measure for objective and subjective poverty

	Cramer's V	R0
Brazil	0.50	0.89
Colombia	0.51	0.94
Ecuador	0.42	0.98
El Salvador	0.61	0.88
Paraguay	0.61	0.84
Peru	0.46	0.63
Uruguay	0.44	0.92

Notes: Objective poverty is measured considering official national poverty lines.

Source: Based on household surveys from Brazil (2017–2018), Colombia (2016–2017), Ecuador (2014), El Salvador (2005–2006), Paraguay (2011–2012), Peru (2018), and Uruguay (2016–2017).

Salvador.[14] The values of the R0 indicate that most households which are poor under the lowest measure of poverty (absolute) are also poor under the subjective measure of poverty. The figures of redundancy range from 0.63 in Peru to 0.98 in Ecuador. In this last case, almost all households classified as poor in absolute terms are also poor in subjective terms, although the opposite does not hold (as the Cramer's V coefficient indicates).

These results indicate that while most objectively poor households also consider themselves poor, there are many households that consider themselves poor but are not classified as such by objective measures. This discrepancy highlights the existence of a population experiencing subjective poverty despite being above the objective poverty threshold, a phenomenon that merits further exploration, and is explored in the following sections.

7 Being Income Nonpoor but Feeling Poor: Determinants

The discrepancies between objective and subjective poverty prevalence may derive from poor indivuals under the objective approach who do not identify themselves as poor, or from nonpoor individuals under the objective approach who feel that they have less than what they need. As discussed in the previous section, in our selected Latin American countries, a significant proportion of nonobjectively poor households lie below the SPL. Given the relevance of this situation, we explore the factors associated to considering poor – that is, being subjectively poor – when the per capita household income is higher than the objective poverty line.

We focus on the universe of households that are nonpoor under the objective poverty measure, and run Probit regressions for subjective poverty in each country. The dependent variable takes the value 1 when the household is classified as poor under the subjective measure, given that it is nonpoor under the objective threshold, and 0 otherwise. As explanatory variables, we choose not to include variables considered in the estimation of the subjective poverty threholds to get a more clear picture of the factors purely associated to the detected divergences in classifications. As independent variables, we explore variables previuosly studied as determinants of subjective poverty. The first set of variables are personal characteristics of household members: if the household head is unemployed, informal, has health insurance, or is inmigrant, and if there is a retired person in the household. The second set of variables refers to housing tenure and conditions, as well as an asset index. The indexes of housing characteristics and assest are both calculated based on Principal Component Analysis. The housing

---

[14] Results corresponding to ECLAC and World Bank poverty lines are similar; they are available upon request to the authors.

conditions index includes the number of rooms if the household has electricity, if the household has drinking water inside the dwelling, if it has sanitation, and if it has electricity or gas for cooking. The asset index considers binary variables that reflect the ownership of specific assets (refrigerator, television, DVD, microwave, computer, car, motorcycle, internet, air conditioning, and washing machine). The third set of determinants refers to the structure of expenditure of the household, taking advantage of the expenditure datasets. In particular, we include a binary variable that indicates if the households spend more than what they earn (in monthly basis). Finally, we include binary variables that indicate if the household is beneficiary of some specific social programs, such as conditional cash transfer programs, labor inclusion programs, or noncontributory pensions.

Our main results are presented in Table A.5, based on national poverty line. The main findings presented in this section are robust to the alternative poverty lines from ECLAC (see Table A.6) and the World Bank (see Table A.7).

The coefficients of the variables reflecting personal charactersitics of household members are presented in Figure 6. As expected, among nonobjective poor households, the probability of subjective poverty increases when the household head is unemployed, although the coefficient is not significat in the case of Uruguay. The same happens in Brazil, Colombia, and Uruguay when the household head is an informal worker, although this result does not hold for Peru. The unemployment coefficients tend to be larger in magnitude compared to the coefficients for informality. This suggests that the link between subjective poverty and economic insecurity is particularly strong for unemployment, altough it also holds for infromality. This can be interpreted as an association between subjective poverty and the economic insecurity derived from unemployment spells or informal jobs.

The effect of the presence of a retired person or pensioner in the households does not show a clear pattern across countries. It is not significant in Ecuador, El Salvador, Paraguay, and Peru, and presents opposite signs in Colombia and Uruguay. In the former, the presence of a retired person is associated with a lower probbablity of being subjectively poor, which is consistent with the idea of the effect of a more permanent or secure income. The result corresponding to Uruguay is puzzling, given the relative high value of pensions when compared to labor income in this country. A simple comparison of objective and subjective poverty incidence by age group in this country indicates that the incidence of subjective poverty is very high among older people, and the contrary happens with objective poverty (see Figure A.1). This result for older people in Uruguay deserves further research. One hypothesis is that it may be associated with the composition of the poverty line basket and the consumption patterns of the elderly, especially spending on medications. Uruguay has universal health

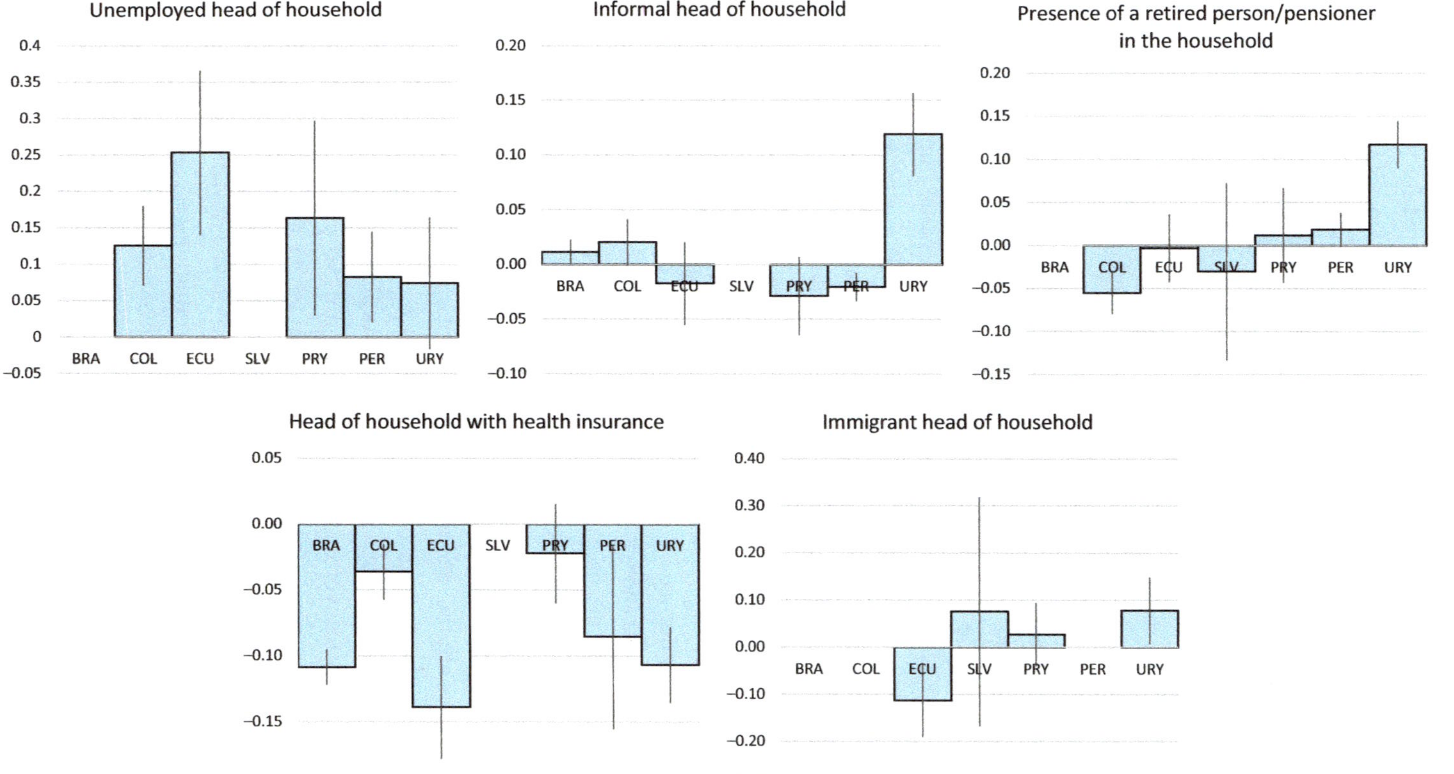

Figure 6 Household characteristics. Marginal effects for the probability of being poor under subjective approach, among households nonpoor under the objective approach.

Note: The regression includes variables that reflect the characteristics of the people in the household, housing and household characteristics, expenditure behavior, participation in social programs, and regional controls. Objective poverty is measured considering official national poverty lines.

Source: Based on household surveys from Brazil (2017–2018), Colombia (2016–2017), Ecuador (2014), El Salvador (2005–2006), Paraguay (2011–2012), Peru (2018), and Uruguay (2016–2017).

coverage, where older adults are typically diagnosed and monitored for their health conditions, potentially leading to higher out-of-pocket medication expenses that may not be fully captured in the objective poverty measure.

In general terms, the probability of subjective poverty is lower in households whose head has health insurance, again a sign of economic security or lower risk of catastrophic expenses as a factor associated with not feeling poor. Only in Paraguay this result is not statistically significant.

Additionally, in Uruguay, the presence of an immigrant household head is associated with a higher probability of subjective poverty, although the size of the coefficient is very small.[15] The opposite happens in Ecuador, while the presence of an immigrant household head is not significant in Paraguay and El Salvador. It is interesting to note that the immigrant background is only significant and positive in the country that can be considered as more developed in our sample. The result for Uruguay is aligned with previous studies that investigate the association between migrant status and subjective poverty in developed countries, which reported that migrants are more likely than nonmigrants to perceive an inability to make ends meet (Buttler 2013; Ayllón & Fusco 2017).

Following previous studies, we also explore the role of housing tenure, housing conditions, and assets on subjective poverty (Figure 7). As expected, households in Brazil, Ecuador, and Paraguay that own their homes outright (with no remaining mortgage) show a lower probability of considering themselves subjectively poor. The effect is not significant in El Salvador and Peru, and contrary to expectations, it presents a positive sign for Colombia and Uruguay. Colombia and Uruguay are the countries with the lowest proportion of homeowners in our sample (Figure A.2). Results for Colombia and Uruguay appear counterintuitive and deserve further exploration. In the case of Uruguay, when we add controls for age brackets in the regression, the coefficient of home ownership becomes not significant. As already discussed, the incidence of subjective poverty is very high among older people (see Figure A.1), who are also more likely to be homeowners. In the case of Colombia, when the variable that reflects if the household spends more than it earns is excluded from the regression, the effect of home ownership becomes negative as expected. Therefore, the counterintuitive results for these countries seem to be driven by the combined effects of home ownership with other variables: in the case of Uruguay, with the age of the household head, and in the case of Colombia, with the variable that reflects if

---

[15] In Uruguay, around 2.5 percent of the population are immigrants in the years close to the survey.

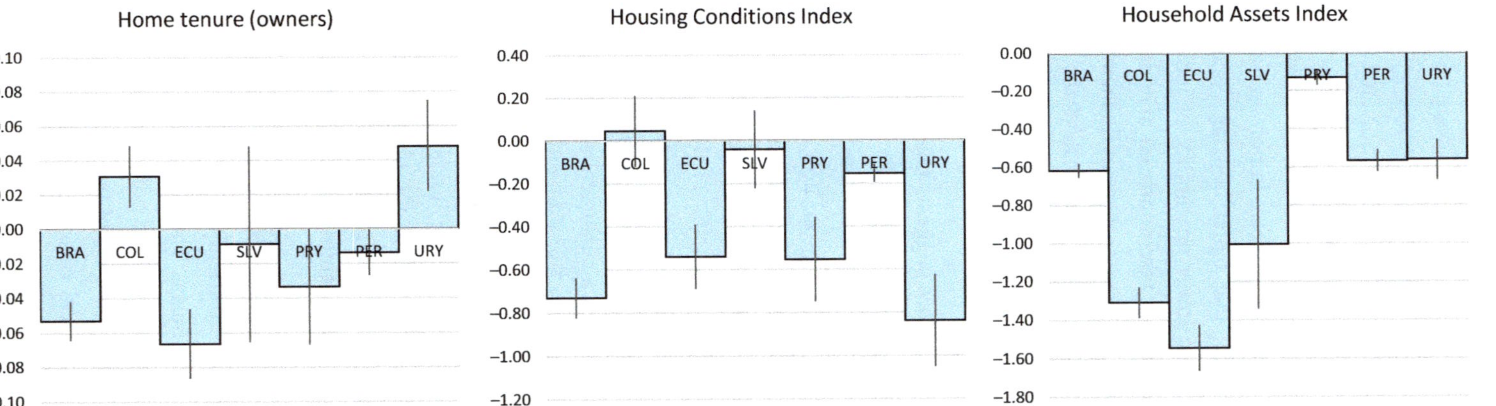

Figure 7 Housing, assets, and savings. Marginal effects for the probability of being poor under subjective approach, among households nonpoor under the objective approach.

Note: The regression includes variables that reflect the characteristics of the people in the household, housing and household characteristics, expenditure behavior, participation in social programs, and regional controls. Objective poverty is measured considering official national poverty lines.

Source: Based on household surveys from Brazil (2017–2018), Colombia (2016–2017), Ecuador (2014), El Salvador (2005–2006), Paraguay (2011–2012), Peru (2018), and Uruguay (2016–2017).

expenditures are higher than earnings. A more thorough understanding of the underlying phenomena requires further research.

The composite index of housing conditions is associated with lower subjective poverty in all countries, except for Colombia and El Salvador. On the same vein, a higher household asset index is associated with lower levels of subjective poverty, and the magnitude of this effect is important for all our considered countries. These findings reflect that better housing conditions and greater household assets are linked to a lower probability of individuals perceiving themselves as poor. This may be because improved material living conditions and valuable possessions provide a greater sense of financial security and well-being, even if the household's income is still near the poverty line. The relatively high coefficients for the asset index indicate that the accumulation of diverse assets plays an important role in shaping subjective perceptions of poverty.

As already discussed, the literature suggests that expenditure patterns play a crucial role in shaping perceptions of poverty. When households spend more than they earn, they face financial deterioration either through reduced savings or increased debt, depending on how they finance the excess expenditure. This overspending may reflect underlying financial difficulties, particularly when households must stretch their resources to cover essential needs or cope with unexpected financial challenges. Such patterns of expenditure exceeding income often signal economic vulnerability. Our analysis across the seven Latin American countries in this study supports these arguments. Figure 8 illustrates a consistent and significant relationship between household spending patterns and subjective poverty assessments. In all seven countries examined, we find that households whose total expenditure exceeds their total income have a markedly higher probability of considering themselves poor. This finding holds true even when we limit our analysis to households that are above the objective poverty line. This relationship is visually represented in Figure 8, which shows the marginal effects of overspending on the probability of subjective poverty for each country.

The consistency of this pattern across diverse national contexts underscores its importance. The magnitude of the effect varies by country, but in all cases, it is positive and statistically significant. This suggests that the experience of spending more than one's income is universally associated with feelings of economic insecurity or hardship, regardless of the specific economic and social context. However, one key analytical constraint is that we cannot determine from our dataset whether such overspending represents a short-term anomaly or

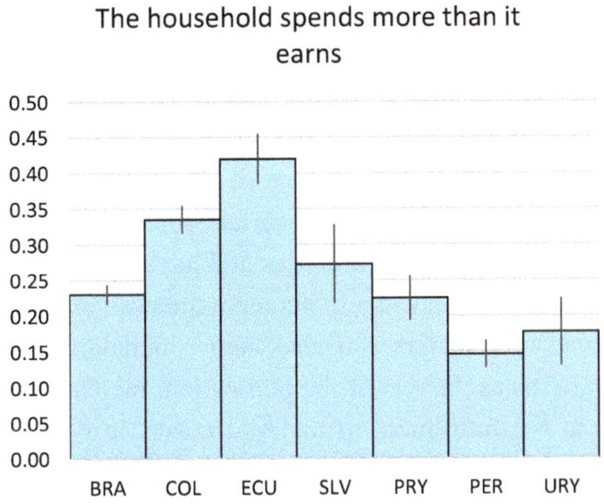

The household spends more than it
earns

BRA COL ECU SLV PRY PER URY

Figure 8 Expenditure. Marginal effects for the probability of being poor under subjective approach, among households nonpoor under the objective approach.

Note: The regression includes variables that reflect the characteristics of the people in the household, housing and household characteristics, expenditure behavior, participation in social programs, and regional controls. Objective poverty is measured considering official national poverty lines.

Source: Based on household surveys from Brazil (2017–2018), Colombia (2016–2017), Ecuador (2014), El Salvador (2005–2006), Paraguay (2011–2012), Peru (2018), and Uruguay (2016–2017).

a chronic condition. The duration of overspending could significantly impact how households evaluate their economic well-being.

It's crucial to emphasize that this analysis focuses on households that are not considered poor by objective standards. This means that the observed imbalance between income and expenditure is not likely to be driven by the necessity to meet basic subsistence needs. Instead, this overspending could be attributed to a variety of factors. These may include unexpected expenses or financial shocks such as medical emergencies or major repairs, lifestyle choices that may exceed current income levels, obligations or expectations that strain the household budget like education costs or supporting extended family, temporary income fluctuations that are not reflected in current expenditure patterns, or access to credit that allows for spending beyond current income.

Given the significance and consistency of the relationship between expenditure patterns and subjective poverty perceptions in all the countries considered in this study, we explore this link more carefully in the following section.

The literature has also discussed the role of social welfare in subjective well-being, referring to the concept of welfare stigma. This stigma reflects the disutility or psychological cost from taking up welfare benefits, associated to the prevalence of negative opinions concerning beneficiaries' deservingness and worth as citizens (Besley & Coate, 1992). If the idea of "undeserving poor" is widespread in a certain society, beneficiaries may be affected by these negative social attitudes and have feelings of social exclusion, leading to a greater tendency to perceive themselves as poor. But at the same time, monetary transfers can also help beneficiaries to have similar consumption patterns as the rest of the population, increase income security, and contribute to the fulfillment of material needs, leading to the opposite effect. This implies that the question about the potential effect of these transfers on subjective well-being remains an open empirical question (Roelen, 2020). We test the presence of this stigma in relation to subjective poverty, considering different policy interventions targeted to the poor: conditional cash transfer programs, labor inclusion programs, and noncontributory pensions. Our results indicate that receiving a conditional cash transfer and, to a lesser extent, being a beneficiary of a labor inclusion program are associated to lower subjective poverty in those countries where this link can be tested (Figure 9). The results corresponding to being beneficiary of a labor inclusion program are not significant. The only exception is the case of noncontributory pensions in Peru, which is associated to a greater probability of being subjective poor.

There are other potential explanations of this result besides the absence of stigma. They are consistent with previous evidence that indicates that beneficiaries of social programs tend not to consider this income when answering the MIQ. Early studies of subjective poverty (Kapteyn et al., 1988) reported that respondents only know approximately their income and answer the MIQ question based on estimates of their actual income. These authors argue that respondents neglect some sources of income, like benefit transfers, when answering the MIQ question. If respondents use an estimate of their actual income as a reference point for their minimum income, not accounting for all their income could bias downward their reported minimum incomes. This would imply that beneficiaries could have lower SPLs, and thus lower subjective poverty than similar households that do not receive these programs, due to the bias in their responses.

Finally, we also examined the role of the poverty gap, recognizing that households may not be objectively poor, but their proximity to the poverty line could lead to subjective feelings of poverty and heightened vulnerability. As anticipated, a higher ratio of per capita household income to the objective

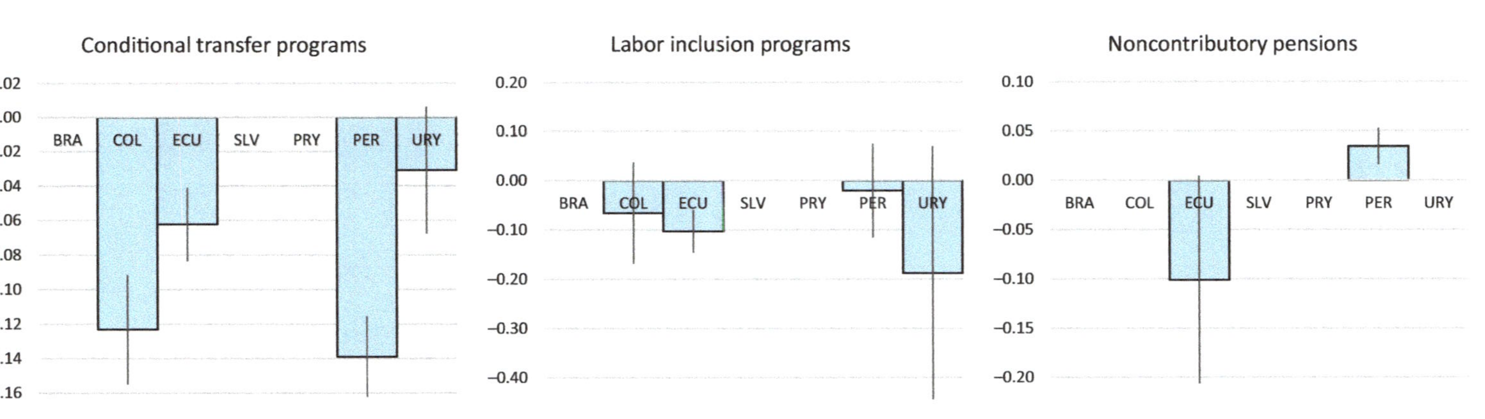

Figure 9 Social assistance. Marginal effects for the probability of being poor under subjective approach, among households nonpoor under the objective approach.

Note: The regression includes variables that reflect the characteristics of the people in the household, housing and household characteristics, expenditure behavior, participation in social programs, and regional controls. Objective poverty is measured considering official national poverty lines.

Source: Based on household surveys from Brazil (2017–2018), Colombia (2016–2017), Ecuador (2014), El Salvador (2005–2006), Paraguay (2011–2012), Peru (2018), and Uruguay (2016–2017).

poverty threshold correlates with a lower likelihood of subjective poverty (Table A.8). Specifically, the closer a household's income is to the poverty line, the more likely they are to perceive themselves as poor, even if they are not technically below the objective threshold. The main findings related to economic insecurity variables remain consistent, albeit with reduced marginal coefficients, and changes in the significance in specific cases, probably reflecting the multicollinearity between personal characteristics of household heads and household income. This result suggests that the effect of being above the poverty line on subjective poverty is heterogeneous and depends on the household's actual income level. Households appear to internalize their material conditions and proximity to the poverty line, which then shapes their subjective perceptions of poverty.

8 Consumption and Subjective Poverty

The discussion in the previous section about the factors associated with the discrepancy between subjective and objective poverty measures highlights the role of income levels, and the relationship between income and consumption, as relevant factors. On that line, the literature suggests that household consumption matters for subjective poverty, not only in terms of level, but also in terms of structure. Consumption patterns may play a key role in mediating the link between objective and subjective poverty measures, and recent studies have examined how expenditure on different types of goods and services can shape an individual's sense of poverty, even when their income is above the official poverty line. Lower consumption of goods related to status signaling may contribute to subjective poverty, while consumption that provides direct utility, like leisure, can mitigate feelings of poverty. It is interesting to note that consumption is underexplored in subjective poverty studies with a purely economic perspective. Most studies on this topic come from sociology, a discipline that assigns social meaning to consumption, either as a way through which individuals construct their identities or a marker of social prestige and status.

Studies utilizing data from the Hong Kong Panel Survey for Poverty Alleviation have revealed distinct consumption clusters and their impacts on perceived poverty status (Peng, 2023; Peng & Law, 2023). The study of Peng (2023) classifies ten consumption categories on two dimensions: conspicuous or non-conspicuous, and experiential or non-experiential. Conspicuous consumption describes the purchase of goods to display social status and economic power, while experiential consumption describes purchases made primarily to acquire a life experience. Results indicate that expenditure on leisure, which falls into both conspicuous and experiential consumption, increases the probability of feeling nonpoor among the economically poor and, conversely, reduces the probability of feeling poor among the economically nonpoor. The analysis also revealed that these relationships were mediated by self-perceived social status (conspicuous consumption pathway) but not by social connectedness (experiential consumption pathway). The findings confirm that the way people spend their money shapes their perceptions of poverty, which may deviate from their poverty status as measured by economic criteria.

In a related analysis, Peng & Law (2023) propose that households allocate their monetary resources into different consumption categories, which may lead to varying levels of utility, thereby shaping their perceptions of poverty in different ways. Their econometric analysis showed that economically poor households with predominantly food-focused spending were less likely to perceive themselves as nonpoor compared to those with balanced spending patterns. Conversely, among nonpoor households, those with high mortgage expenditures were more likely to feel poor than those with balanced spending. Interestingly, when researchers accounted for asset ownership in their analysis, the relationship between high mortgage payments and subjective feelings of poverty disappeared. This suggests that any negative perceptions associated with high mortgage costs may be counterbalanced by the psychological benefits of owning property and other assets.[16]

Building upon these insights about consumption patterns and subjective poverty, we next analyze the situation of Latin American countries, focusing on overspending and consumption patterns. Our previous regression analysis showed that, among nonpoor households, those whose total expenditure exceeds their total income have a higher probability of considering themselves poor. When we consider all households, we find that in all countries, households that are poor by both criteria show the highest proportion of overspenders, followed by households that are not objectively poor but are poor according to subjective measurement (Figure 10). This trend illustrates that the discrepancy between income and expenditure – that is, the insufficiency of economic means to achieve desired consumption goals – plays a fundamental

---

[16] Other studies analyzed consumption patterns focusing on subjective well-being or happiness, instead of subjective poverty. Noll & Weick (2015) for Germany found that expenditures on clothing and leisure are drivers of subjective well-being, while expenditures on food and housing do not affect life satisfaction significantly. Similarly, a study by DeLeire and Kalil (2010) on older Americans found that only leisure consumption was positively related to happiness, while health and communication expenditures had negative or insignificant effects.

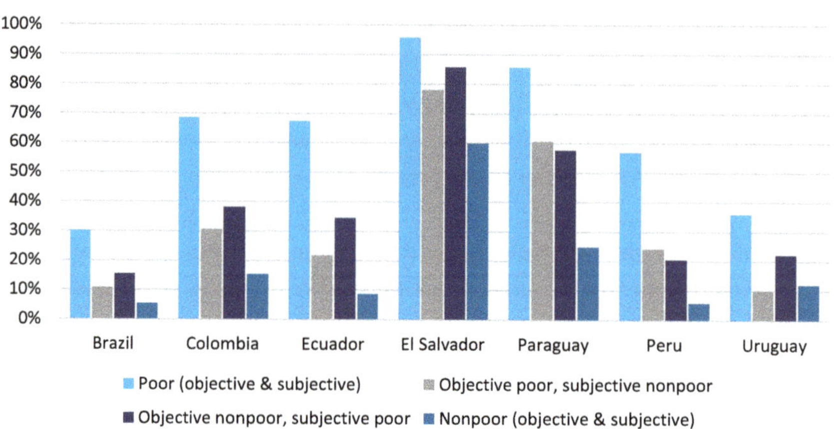

Figure 10 Households with overspending (expenditure higher than income).

Source: Based on household surveys from Brazil (2017–2018), Colombia (2016–2017), Ecuador (2014), El Salvador (2005–2006), Paraguay (2011–2012), Peru (2018), and Uruguay (2016–2017).

role in self-perception of poverty, beyond the established objective income thresholds.

In economic terms, when expenditures exceed income, it results in dissaving or a reduction in net worth. This can lead to accumulating debt if the deficit is financed through borrowing, or depleting savings if the extra spending is funded from previously accumulated assets. In the context of poverty research and household economics, this situation is often an indicator of financial stress or economic vulnerability, especially if it persists over time. It can be a sign that the household is struggling to meet its basic needs with its current income, or that there are unexpected expenses or financial shocks that the household is dealing with. As already discussed, our data do not allow us to distinguish whether this imbalance is a temporary phenomenon or a persistent state for these households. This limitation is important to note as the duration and frequency of overspending could have different implications for subjective poverty assessments.

An initial descriptive analysis of consumption patterns among households that are not poor in objective terms reveals interesting differences between those who consider themselves subjectively poor and those who do not. The patterns detected are generally present across all countries, although in El Salvador's case, some are not statistically significant. The proportion of spending on food and dwelling is higher among households that are not objectively poor but feel poor, while expenditures on recreation, communication, and culture tend to be lower (Table 7). They also tend to have a lower proportion of consumption of

Table 7 Expenditure shares by component, among nonpoor households in objective terms

	Brazil			Colombia			Ecuador			El Salvador		
	Sub. nonpoor	Sub. poor	*p*-value	Sub. nonpoor	Sub. poor	*p*-value	Sub. nonpoor	Sub. poor	*p*-value	Sub. nonpoor	Sub. poor	*p*-value
Food	17%	21%	0.000	17%	19%	0.000	29%	36%	0.000	28%	29%	0.158
Alcohol and tobacco	1%	1%	0.000	1%	1%	0.013	2%	1%	0.000			
Clothes	5%	5%	0.000	4%	3%	0.000	4%	3%	0.000	4%	4%	0.002
Dwelling	22%	29%	0.000	32%	40%	0.000	17%	21%	0.000	26%	29%	0.000
Household	8%	7%	0.000	4%	3%	0.000	5%	5%	0.000	6%	6%	0.130
Health	9%	8%	0.000	1%	1%	0.174	5%	4%	0.003	5%	4%	0.265
Education	3%	2%	0.000	2%	1%	0.000	5%	3%	0.000	2%	2%	0.036
Transport	12%	9%	0.000	9%	6%	0.000	12%	8%	0.000	5%	3%	0.004
Comunication	4%	3%	0.000	4%	3%	0.000	3%	2%	0.000	3%	3%	0.018
Recreation and culture	3%	2%	0.000	3%	2%	0.000	3%	2%	0.000	4%	3%	0.309
Restaurants and hotels	6%	4%	0.000	8%	8%	0.098	11%	9%	0.000	7%	7%	0.011
Other	10%	9%	0.000	15%	11%	0.000	4%	4%	0.000	10%	9%	0.005

Table 7 (cont.)

	Paraguay			Peru			Uruguay		
	Sub. nonpoor	Sub. poor	*p*-value	Sub. nonpoor	Sub. poor	*p*-value	Sub. nonpoor	Sub. poor	*p*-value
Food	31%	32%	0.084	40%	40%	0.051	**21%**	**27%**	**0.000**
Alcohol and tobacco	1%	1%	0.553	0%	0%	0.008	1%	1%	0.368
Clothes	**3%**	**3%**	**0.000**	**6%**	**4%**	**0.000**	**4%**	**3%**	**0.000**
Dwelling	**21%**	**28%**	**0.000**	**22%**	**29%**	**0.000**	**30%**	**37%**	**0.000**
Household	6%	6%	0.182	5%	5%	0.048	**4%**	**3%**	**0.000**
Health	5%	4%	0.002	**5%**	**4%**	**0.000**	5%	5%	0.054
Education	**2%**	**2%**	**0.000**	**3%**	**1%**	**0.000**	**2%**	**0%**	**0.000**
Transport	**11%**	**8%**	**0.000**	**5%**	**4%**	**0.000**	**11%**	**6%**	**0.000**
Comunication	**5%**	**4%**	**0.000**	**4%**	**4%**	**0.000**	5%	5%	0.415
Recreation and culture	3%	3%	0.002	**3%**	**2%**	**0.000**	**7%**	**6%**	**0.000**
Restaurants and hotels	6%	5%	0.178	**2%**	**2%**	**0.000**	**3%**	**2%**	**0.000**
Other	6%	5%	0.000	**5%**	**5%**	**0.000**	6%	6%	0.002

Source: Based on household surveys from Brazil (2017–2018), Colombia (2016–2017), Ecuador (2014), El Salvador (2005–2006), Paraguay (2011–2012), Peru (2018), and Uruguay (2016–2017).

services like education, health, and transport. These spending patterns suggest a constrained lifestyle where basic needs take precedence over investments in human capital and quality of life. Consistent with previous findings for other regions, our results indicate that in Latin America households that allocate a larger share of their budget to basic necessities like food and housing, leaving less room for discretionary spending on leisure and cultural activities, tend to perceive themselves as poor despite having income levels above the objective poverty threshold.

To more rigorously analyze the relationship between consumption patterns and subjective poverty, we estimate a probit model similar to the one discussed in the previous section (Section 7), but incorporating variables related to the proportion of different consumption items. As in the previous section, this probit model focuses on households that are not poor in objective terms and investigates the factors associated with their self-perception as poor. In addition to all the variables included in the previous version of the estimation, we alternatively add variables indicating the proportion of household expenditure on different consumption items. Each proportion is included separately in a new estimation. Table 8 presents the main results of interest, showing how the proportion of spending on specific consumption items is associated with the probability that a household with income above the poverty line considers itself poor (i.e., is classified as subjectively poor). Each row corresponds to a separate estimation as the spending proportions are included individually rather than simultaneously. The coefficients for the control variables analyzed in the previous section remain stable across these specifications.[17]

Two types of consumption are associated with a higher probability of objectively nonpoor population feeling poor: a higher proportion of food and beverage expenditure and, especially, a higher proportion of dwelling expenditure (Table 8). The positive association between higher dwelling expenditure and subjective poverty is considerable in magnitude and significant across all countries, except for El Salvador. The positive association between the proportion spent on food and beverages is present in Brazil, Colombia, Ecuador, and Uruguay, while not significant in El Salvador and Paraguay, and shows a negative sign in Peru. These results reflect that a high proportion of spending on basic necessities like food and housing might signal economic constraints even among households above the poverty line. The strong relationship between dwelling expenditure and subjective poverty could indicate that housing costs represent a significant financial burden that shapes households' perceptions of

---

[17] These results are available upon request.

Table 8 Expenditure shares by component, among nonpoor households in objective terms

	Brazil	Colombia	Ecuador	El Salvador	Paraguay	Peru	Uruguay
Prop. of expenditure in food and drinks	0.065*** (0.016)	0.193*** (0.036)	0.537*** (0.034)	−0.075 (0.096)	−0.123* (0.065)	−0.151*** (0.019)	0.385*** (0.050)
Prop. of expenditure in alcohol and tobacco	0.048 (0.064)	−0.690*** (0.160)	−1.152*** (0.123)	–	−0.629** (0.310)	−0.627*** (0.220)	−0.195 (0.208)
Prop. of expenditure in clothing	−0.340*** (0.049)	−0.642*** (0.091)	−0.737*** (0.100)	−0.921*** (0.324)	−1.122*** (0.273)	−0.657*** (0.076)	−0.951*** (0.193)
Prop. of expenditure in dwelling	0.301*** (0.015)	0.849*** (0.031)	0.779*** (0.049)	0.419*** (0.095)	0.746*** (0.064)	0.492*** (0.022)	0.337*** (0.040)
Prop. of expenditure in household	−0.134*** (0.033)	−0.229** (0.113)	−0.405*** (0.091)	−0.166 (0.275)	−0.075 (0.184)	0.035 (0.080)	−0.843*** (0.136)

Prop. of expenditure in health	−0.126*** (0.025)	0.138 (0.121)	−0.229*** (0.061)	−0.026 (0.202)	−0.050 (0.167)	−0.214*** (0.040)	−0.202* (0.115)
Prop. of expenditure in education	−0.086** (0.042)	−0.535*** (0.101)	−0.231*** (0.083)	−0.298 (0.438)	−0.346 (0.230)	−0.400*** (0.068)	−0.809*** (0.212)
Prop. of expenditure in transport	−0.251*** (0.023)	−0.643*** (0.059)	−0.610*** (0.046)	0.095 (0.181)	−0.614*** (0.110)	−0.111** (0.056)	−0.518*** (0.076)
Prop. of expenditure in comunication	−0.105* (0.056)	−0.029 (0.139)	−1.891*** (0.200)	−0.595 (0.460)	−0.381* (0.219)	0.048 (0.080)	0.240 (0.194)
Prop. of expenditure in recreation	−0.313*** (0.075)	−0.223* (0.115)	−0.537*** (0.086)	−0.003 (0.242)	−0.078 (0.375)	−0.495*** (0.104)	−0.507*** (0.118)
Prop. of expenditure in restaurant and hotels	−0.304*** (0.038)	−0.260*** (0.048)	−0.395*** (0.046)	−0.075 (0.189)	−0.316*** (0.120)	−0.095* (0.056)	−0.648*** (0.151)
Prop. of other expenditure	−0.128*** (0.031)	−0.838*** (0.046)	−0.492*** (0.135)	−0.509*** (0.178)	−0.746*** (0.216)	−0.133** (0.067)	−0.350*** (0.118)

Robust standard errors in parentheses

*** $p < 0.01$, ** $p < 0.05$, * $p < 0.1$

Source: Based on household surveys from Brazil (2017–2018), Colombia (2016–2017), Ecuador (2014), El Salvador (2005–2006), Paraguay (2011–2012), Peru (2018), and Uruguay (2016–2017).

their economic well-being, even when their absolute income levels suggest otherwise. It is important to notice that the strong association corresponding to the proportion of spending on dwelling is clear and significant, even if we are controlling for household assets and other household characteristics.

Consumption expenditures are more associated with conspicuous or experiential spending, such as clothing, recreation, restaurants and hotels, and communication, and are negatively related to the probability of feeling poor. Similarly, expenditures on health, education, and transport, which involve out-of-pocket or private spending beyond what might be derived from public services, are also associated with a lower probability of feeling poor. These findings align with recent research on subjective well-being and consumption patterns, suggesting that the ability to engage in discretionary spending beyond basic necessities plays a crucial role in how households perceive their economic status.

The negative association between subjective poverty and these types of expenditures could be explained by several factors. First, the ability to allocate resources to conspicuous consumption may serve as a signal of social status, both to others and to oneself. Second, experiential purchases, such as recreation and dining out, often contribute to social connection and life satisfaction, potentially offsetting feelings of economic hardship. Third, the capacity to access private services in health, education, and transportation might indicate a level of choice and control over one's consumption decisions, rather than being constrained to rely solely on public services. This suggests that the relationship between consumption patterns and subjective poverty goes beyond simple income-expenditure calculations, incorporating aspects of lifestyle quality and future economic prospects.

9 Policy Implications and Final Remarks

Poverty studies in the economics field are dominated by the objective approach, and within this approach, by monetary measures of poverty. Given the strong technical assumptions needed for the setting of an objective poverty threshold, there is a case for complementing the analysis originated by expert-derived poverty thresholds with views which consider the insider's perspectives and people's perceptions about their own poverty status. The combination of both approaches has the potential to provide a more comprehensive view of poverty and exclusion.

Since the early beginnings of the study of subjective poverty (Van Praag, 1968), the literature in this area has grown significantly and findings from subjective-based measures have broadened our understanding about poverty.

Most of this literature is focused on developed countries. In Latin America, some recent expenditure surveys include the question about the minimum income needed for the household to make ends meet. This information allows to derive a poverty line in the income space, defined as the income level at which some critical level of subjective welfare is reached. Taking advantage of this information, we compare monetary objective and subjective measures of poverty in seven Latin American countries and analyze potential divergencies between both poverty profiles.

Our study contributes to the understanding of poverty in Latin America by comparing objective and subjective poverty measures across seven countries. Our results reveal systematic differences between objective and subjective approaches to poverty measurement, with subjective thresholds consistently higher than objective ones. Consequently, subjective poverty levels exceed objective poverty rates across all studied countries, with the gap ranging from minimal differences in Peru, Paraguay, and El Salvador to significant divergences of around 20 percentage points in Brazil, Colombia, and Uruguay, reaching up to 38 points in Ecuador.

A key finding is that a substantial proportion of households classified as nonpoor by objective standards consider themselves poor. This discrepancy is particularly concentrated among households in the second and third quintiles of the income distribution, suggesting that middle-income households often experience a sense of economic vulnerability despite being above official poverty thresholds. Our analysis reveals that this subjective assessment of poverty is strongly associated with factors reflecting economic insecurity, including unemployment, labor informality, and lack of health insurance. Additionally, housing conditions, asset ownership, and the ability to maintain balanced household finances play crucial roles in shaping perceptions of poverty. The systematic prevalence of these patterns across countries, despite their different socioeconomic contexts, underscores the structural nature of this phenomenon in Latin America.

The study also uncovers important insights about consumption patterns and their relationship to subjective poverty. Households that allocate a larger share of their budget to basic necessities like food and housing, leaving less room for discretionary spending, tend to perceive themselves as poor despite having income levels above the objective poverty threshold. Notably, households whose expenditures exceed their income show a higher probability of feeling poor, highlighting the significance of financial stability in subjective well-being. This relationship between consumption patterns and subjective poverty goes beyond simple income–expenditure calculations, incorporating aspects of lifestyle quality and future economic prospects. As found in previous studies for other regions, leisure expenditure (including spending on cultural, sports, social entertainment, and self-entertainment activities) is a significant predictor of subjective poverty among the economically nonpoor.

Our findings suggest that traditional poverty alleviation strategies focused solely on raising incomes may be insufficient to address the complex nature of perceived economic hardship. Instead, policy approaches should extend to address broader aspects of economic security. This includes strengthening social protection systems to better address economic vulnerability, particularly for households just above the objective poverty line. The development of policies to promote formal employment and expand health insurance coverage emerges as a crucial component, given the strong association between these factors and subjective poverty. Furthermore, the implementation of programs to improve financial literacy and household budget management could help households better manage their resources and reduce their vulnerability to economic shocks.

The significant relationship between housing conditions, asset ownership, and subjective poverty underscores the importance of policies that facilitate asset accumulation and improve housing conditions, even among households above the poverty line. The expansion of access to affordable housing programs and the creation of incentives for household savings and asset building could help reduce feelings of economic insecurity. Additionally, programs focused on improving housing quality and basic infrastructure could contribute to enhancing households' perceived economic well-being.

The reception of conditional cash transfers and participation in labor inclusion programs are associated with lower subjective poverty in those countries where this link could be tested. This suggests that social protection programs may play a role in reducing subjective poverty beyond their direct income effects, possibly through providing greater economic security and stability. However, the relationship between social programs and subjective poverty merits further investigation, particularly regarding the mechanisms through which these programs might influence perceptions of economic well-being.

The discrepancies between objective and subjective poverty measures observed in this study suggest that traditional income-based approaches may be overlooking crucial aspects of household well-being. This indicates the value of incorporating subjective measures in poverty assessment and policy design. The consistent finding across countries that economic insecurity factors strongly influence subjective poverty, even among households above objective poverty thresholds, suggests the need for a more comprehensive approach to poverty measurement and alleviation.

Future research could benefit from longitudinal studies to better understand the causal relationships between economic insecurity and subjective poverty. Such studies could help identify how changes in employment status, health insurance coverage, asset ownership, and consumption patterns over time influence perceptions of poverty. Additionally, qualitative research could provide deeper insights into how households evaluate their economic well-being and what factors they consider most important in these assessments.

The results for Peru and Ecuador, which show particularly interesting patterns in the relationship between objective and subjective poverty, deserve special attention in future research. Understanding why these countries deviate in some cases from regional patterns could provide valuable insights into the factors that influence subjective poverty assessments and the effectiveness of different policy approaches.

In the Latin American context, where economic insecurity and vulnerability are persistent concerns, our findings emphasize the importance of developing comprehensive policy approaches that address not only absolute income levels but also the broader factors that influence households' perceived economic well-being. The strong relationship between economic insecurity and subjective poverty suggests that policies aimed at reducing vulnerability and increasing stability could be as important as those focused on raising incomes. This more nuanced understanding of poverty could contribute to more effective and targeted poverty reduction strategies in the region.

The integration of subjective poverty measures into policy design and evaluation could help ensure that interventions address not only material deprivation but also the psychological and social aspects of poverty that influence how households perceive their economic situation. This comprehensive approach to poverty alleviation, considering both objective and subjective dimensions, may be more effective in improving the overall well-being of Latin American households.

Appendix

Table A.1 Social and labor market indicators

		Year	Poverty incidence (ECLAC)	Gini coefficient	Female labor force participation	Unemployment rate	Human development Index
Brazil	2017–2018	2017	21.2	0.532	59.45	12,8	0,758
Colombia	2016–2017	2016	29.7	0.518	53.51	8,6	0,763
Ecuador	2013–2014	2013	26.4	0.470	56.09	3,0	0,755
El Salvador	2005–2006	2005	51.6	0.504	43.15	7,2	0,640
Paraguay	2011–2012	2011	31.6	0.535	55.13	5,5	0,711
Peru	2018	2018	16.8	0.439	63.80	3,9	0,770
Uruguay	2016–2017	2016	3.6	0.391	57.56	7,8	0,811

Source: ECLAC Stat, World Bank Indicators and UNDP.

Table A.2 Estimation of subjective poverty lines. Dependent variable: MIQ (log)

	Brazil 2017–2018	Colombia 2016–2017	Ecuador 2013–2014	El Salvador 2005–2006	Paraguay 2011–2012	Peru 2018	Uruguay 2016–2017
Household income (logs)	0.398***	0.059***	0.290***	0.066***	0.088***	0.310***	0.163***
	(0.004)	(0.002)	(0.005)	(0.007)	(0.012)	(0.006)	(0.014)
Number of members	0.025***	0.025***	0.004*	0.044***	0.042***	0.008***	0.027***
	(0.002)	(0.002)	(0.003)	(0.006)	(0.006)	(0.003)	(0.007)
Age of household head	0.012***	0.017***	0.021***	0.024***	0.024***	0.017***	0.021***
	(0.001)	(0.001)	(0.001)	(0.003)	(0.004)	(0.001)	(0.002)
Square of age of household head	−0.000***	−0.000***	−0.000***	−0.000***	−0.000***	−0.000***	−0.000***
	(0.000)	(0.000)	(0.000)	(0.000)	(0.000)	(0.000)	(0.000)
Female household head	−0.034***	−0.022***	−0.085***	0.054*	0.020	−0.036***	−0.076***
	(0.005)	(0.005)	(0.011)	(0.028)	(0.023)	(0.010)	(0.013)
Non-white household head	−0.046***	−0.029***	−0.059***	—	−0.210***	−0.022	−0.061***
	(0.005)	(0.006)	(0.019)		(0.022)	(0.019)	(0.020)
Urban	0.147***	0.351***	0.192***	0.253***	0.240***	0.226***	0.115***
	(0.006)	(0.012)	(0.007)	(0.023)	(0.021)	(0.009)	(0.015)

Marital status of household head

Single	—	—	—	—	—	—	—
Union	—	0.049***	0.085***	0.098**	0.106***	−0.017	0.055
		(0.008)	(0.018)	(0.039)	(0.037)	(0.020)	(0.035)
Married	—	0.157***	0.089***	0.223***	0.155***	0.040**	0.057***
		(0.009)	(0.018)	(0.037)	(0.036)	(0.020)	(0.018)
Separated/divorced	—	0.018**	0.057***	0.048	0.074	0.029*	0.029
		(0.007)	(0.014)	(0.036)	(0.047)	(0.017)	(0.019)
Widow	—	0.076***	0.030*	0.053	0.069	−0.005	0.036
		(0.010)	(0.017)	(0.039)	(0.044)	(0.018)	(0.025)

Houshold type

Unipersonal	—	—	—	—	—	—	—
Single parent	0.050***	0.051***	0.105***	0.219***	0.032	0.075***	0.154***
	(0.010)	(0.008)	(0.016)	(0.048)	(0.043)	(0.015)	(0.024)
Couple without children	0.112***	0.073***	0.048**	0.180***	0.018	−0.008	0.207***
	(0.009)	(0.010)	(0.020)	(0.058)	(0.051)	(0.019)	(0.022)
Couple with children	0.127***	0.086***	0.121***	0.209***	0.082*	0.101***	0.280***
	(0.010)	(0.009)	(0.018)	(0.049)	(0.043)	(0.018)	(0.027)

Table A.2 (cont.)

	Brazil 2017–2018	Colombia 2016–2017	Ecuador 2013–2014	El Salvador 2005–2006	Paraguay 2011–2012	Peru 2018	Uruguay 2016–2017
Extended (nonrelatives)	0.069***	0.154***	0.115***	0.285***	0.213***	0.036	0.184***
	(0.024)	(0.013)	(0.034)	(0.067)	(0.058)	(0.028)	(0.056)
Extended (relatives)	0.074***	0.062***	0.099***	0.214***	0.059	0.022	0.192***
	(0.010)	(0.009)	(0.017)	(0.046)	(0.043)	(0.016)	(0.028)
Education (years)							
No education	–	–	–	–	–	–	–
1 year	0.004	0.071***	−0.000	0.070	0.089	0.075***	−0.078
	(0.013)	(0.016)	(0.029)	(0.050)	(0.138)	(0.022)	(0.072)
2 years	−0.009	0.121***	0.062***	0.090**	0.138	0.092***	0.037
	(0.016)	(0.014)	(0.021)	(0.040)	(0.134)	(0.020)	(0.058)
3 years	−0.002	0.148***	0.086***	0.150***	0.177	0.139***	0.006
	(0.013)	(0.013)	(0.019)	(0.043)	(0.131)	(0.020)	(0.048)
4 years	0.009	0.179***	0.107***	0.141***	0.193	0.157***	−0.005
	(0.012)	(0.014)	(0.021)	(0.048)	(0.132)	(0.023)	(0.048)
5 years	0.070***	0.244***	0.152***	0.179***	0.180	0.191***	0.022
	(0.010)	(0.011)	(0.024)	(0.053)	(0.133)	(0.017)	(0.057)
6 years	0.081***	0.284***	0.173***	0.216***	0.283**	0.209***	0.101**

	(0.012)	(0.014)	(0.014)	(0.035)	(0.130)	(0.020)	(0.042)
7 years	0.116***	0.314***	0.185***	0.325***	0.335**	0.274***	0.199***
	(0.014)	(0.013)	(0.027)	(0.076)	(0.136)	(0.026)	(0.054)
8 years	0.110***	0.312***	0.242***	0.345***	0.382***	0.291***	0.268***
	(0.014)	(0.014)	(0.022)	(0.056)	(0.137)	(0.023)	(0.046)
9 years	0.163***	0.374***	0.270***	0.331***	0.433***	0.362***	0.229***
	(0.011)	(0.014)	(0.019)	(0.038)	(0.132)	(0.022)	(0.045)
10 years	0.156***	0.348***	0.233***	0.290***	0.370***	0.360***	0.317***
	(0.017)	(0.016)	(0.024)	(0.073)	(0.138)	(0.029)	(0.053)
11 years	0.220***	0.465***	0.255***	0.380***	0.424***	0.462***	0.318***
	(0.017)	(0.011)	(0.026)	(0.080)	(0.140)	(0.017)	(0.054)
12 years	0.278***	0.493***	0.352***	0.587***	0.500***	0.550***	0.360***
	(0.010)	(0.026)	(0.017)	(0.038)	(0.132)	(0.028)	(0.048)
13 years	0.397***	0.645***	0.405***	0.876***	0.622***	0.616***	0.420***
	(0.018)	(0.021)	(0.033)	(0.121)	(0.144)	(0.027)	(0.057)
14 years	0.443***	0.514***	0.452***	0.889***	0.593***	0.643***	0.524***
	(0.020)	(0.018)	(0.022)	(0.074)	(0.142)	(0.020)	(0.054)
15 years	0.430***	0.582***	0.566***	0.788***	0.674***	0.740***	0.487***
	(0.020)	(0.013)	(0.026)	(0.052)	(0.138)	(0.034)	(0.053)
16 years	0.576***	0.636***	0.594***	0.972***	0.734***	0.792***	0.506***
	(0.012)	(0.014)	(0.024)	(0.112)	(0.137)	(0.020)	(0.051)

Table A.2 (cont.)

	Brazil 2017–2018	Colombia 2016–2017	Ecuador 2013–2014	El Salvador 2005–2006	Paraguay 2011–2012	Peru 2018	Uruguay 2016–2017
17 years	–	0.688***	0.629***	1.171***	0.841***	0.907***	0.588***
		(0.020)	(0.034)	(0.054)	(0.147)	(0.037)	(0.060)
18 years or more	–	0.948***	0.739***	1.416***	1.017***	1.024***	0.645***
		(0.012)	(0.035)	(0.113)	(0.141)	(0.029)	(0.058)
	3.856***	11.968***	3.675***	3.814***	11.898***	3.770***	7.527***
Constant	(0.036)	(0.030)	(0.045)	(0.095)	(0.220)	(0.057)	(0.141)
Observations	58,037	85,945	28,970	4,380	5,145	33,900	6,880
R-squared	0.475	0.270	0.436	0.366	0.336	0.433	0.361

Standard errors in parentheses // *** $p < 0.01$, ** $p < 0.05$, * $p < 0.1$.

Source: Based on household surveys.

Table A.3 Subjective and objective poverty overlap, by region

			Objective poverty					
			Poor			Nonpoor		
			Urban	Rural	Total	Urban	Rural	Total
Brazil	Subjective poverty	Poor	10.0%	23.9%	12.0%	20.5%	11.9%	19.3%
		Nonpoor	0.8%	5.7%	1.5%	68.7%	58.5%	67.3%
Colombia	Subjective poverty	Poor	31.9%	46.0%	33.3%	27.5%	21.1%	26.8%
		Nonpoor	2.2%	4.0%	2.4%	38.3%	28.8%	37.4%
Ecuador	Subjective poverty	Poor	8.7%	25.9%	14.1%	41.1%	32.3%	38.3%
		Nonpoor	0.1%	0.8%	0.3%	50.2%	41.0%	47.3%
El Salvador	Subjective poverty	Poor	44.1%	65.6%	52.1%	15.8%	4.6%	11.7%
		Nonpoor	5.2%	10.3%	7.1%	34.8%	19.5%	29.1%
Paraguay	Subjective poverty	Poor	20.4%	36.7%	26.8%	16.4%	9.9%	13.8%
		Nonpoor	3.7%	6.1%	4.7%	59.5%	47.3%	54.7%
Peru	Subjective poverty	Poor	11.9%	27.5%	16.3%	12.0%	9.6%	11.4%
		Nonpoor	7.2%	15.5%	9.5%	68.8%	47.5%	62.9%
Uruguay	Subjective poverty	Poor	9.2%	4.3%	8.4%	22.2%	27.3%	23.0%
		Nonpoor	1.7%	0.1%	1.4%	67.0%	68.3%	67.2%

Source: Based on household surveys.

Table A.4 Proportion of subjectively poor, within those households that are not objectively poor

	Brazil	Colombia	Ecuador	El Salvador	Paraguay	Peru	Uruguay
Quintile 1	21.2%	0.0%	13.3%	0.0%	0.0%	0.9%	27.6%
Quintile 2	40.6%	20.4%	39.9%	0.0%	25.2%	38.1%	38.5%
Quintile 3	25.2%	38.8%	26.4%	4.9%	43.5%	32.5%	23.0%
Quintile 4	11.7%	28.3%	15.2%	63.8%	22.4%	19.1%	9.3%
Quintile 5	1.4%	12.5%	5.1%	31.3%	8.9%	9.4%	1.6%

Source: Based on household surveys.

Table A.5 Dependent variable: Probability of being subjectively poor, within those households that are not objectively poor. National poverty line (marginal effects)

	Brazil	Colombia	Ecuador	El Salvador	Paraguay	Peru	Uruguay
Characteristics of the people in the household							
Unemployed head of household	–	0.121***	0.222***	–	0.171***	0.072**	0.082*
		(0.028)	(0.062)		(0.065)	(0.030)	(0.046)
Informal head of household	0.015***	0.021*	−0.001	–	−0.038**	−0.020***	0.117***
	(0.006)	(0.011)	(0.020)		(0.018)	(0.007)	(0.019)
Presence of a retired person/pensioner in the home	–	−0.057***	−0.011	−0.031	0.000	0.016	0.117***
		(0.012)	(0.022)	(0.053)	(0.028)	(0.010)	(0.014)
Head of household with health insurance	−0.108***	−0.036***	−0.100***	–	−0.024	−0.087**	−0.109***
	(0.007)	(0.011)	(0.021)		(0.019)	(0.036)	(0.015)
Immigrant head of household	–	–	−0.125***	0.109	0.022	–	0.077**
			(0.039)	(0.126)	(0.034)		(0.035)
Housing and household characteristics							
Home tenure (owners)	−0.037***	0.025***	−0.049***	−0.045	−0.030*	−0.022***	0.036***
	(0.006)	(0.009)	(0.011)	(0.028)	(0.017)	(0.007)	(0.013)
Housing Conditions Index	−0.747***	0.042	−0.644***	−0.050	−0.569***	−0.162***	−0.855***
	(0.048)	(0.082)	(0.078)	(0.092)	(0.098)	(0.021)	(0.108)
Household Assets Index	−0.581***	−1.321***	−1.594***	−0.888***	−0.139***	−0.577***	−0.589***
	(0.019)	(0.040)	(0.064)	(0.173)	(0.021)	(0.030)	(0.054)

Table **A.5** (cont.)

	Brazil	Colombia	Ecuador	El Salvador	Paraguay	Peru	Uruguay
Expenditure variables							
The household spends more than it earns	0.216***	0.340***	0.444***	0.293***	0.223***	0.195***	0.172***
	(0.010)	(0.010)	(0.014)	(0.031)	(0.016)	(0.009)	(0.017)
Social programs							
Conditional transfer programs	–	−0.124***	−0.066***	–	–	−0.135***	−0.025
		(0.016)	(0.011)			(0.012)	(0.019)
Labor inclusion programs	–	−0.071	−0.093***	–	–	−0.027	−0.180
		(0.053)	(0.022)			(0.049)	(0.133)
Noncontributory pensions	–	–	−0.106**	–	–	0.026***	–
			(0.054)			(0.009)	
Regional controls	Yes	Yes	Yes	Yes	Yes	Yes	Yes
Observations	48,394	55,508	23,389	1,855	3,527	24,730	5,905

Robust standard errors in parentheses.

*** $p < 0.01$, ** $p < 0.05$, * $p < 0.1$.

Source: Based on household surveys.

Table A.6 Dependent variable: Probability of being subjectively poor, within those households that are not objectively poor. ECLAC poverty line (marginal effects)

	Brazil	Colombia	Ecuador	El Salvador	Paraguay	Peru	Uruguay
Characteristics of the people in the household							
Unemployed head of household	–	0.121***	0.247***	–	0.212***	0.086***	0.125***
		(0.026)	(0.059)		(0.067)	(0.033)	(0.043)
Informal head of household	0.024***	0.018*	–0.008	–	–0.022	–0.018***	0.139***
	(0.006)	(0.010)	(0.020)		(0.019)	(0.007)	(0.019)
Presence of a retired person/pensioner in the home	–	–0.056***	0.001	–0.030	0.002	0.017*	0.122***
		(0.012)	(0.020)	(0.053)	(0.030)	(0.011)	(0.014)
Head of household with health insurance	–0.125***	–0.028***	–0.116***	–	–0.017	–0.089**	–0.131***
	(0.007)	(0.010)	(0.021)		(0.020)	(0.035)	(0.015)
Immigrant head of household	–	–	–0.117***	0.076	0.011	–	0.079**
			(0.040)	(0.124)	(0.038)		(0.038)
Housing and household characteristics							
Home tenure (owners)	–0.053***	0.025***	–0.061***	–0.009	–0.038**	–0.017**	0.040***
	(0.006)	(0.009)	(0.010)	(0.029)	(0.018)	(0.007)	(0.014)

Table **A.6** (cont.)

	Brazil	Colombia	Ecuador	El Salvador	Paraguay	Peru	Uruguay
Housing Conditions Index	−0.691***	0.035	−0.608***	−0.039	−0.598***	−0.157***	−0.892***
	(0.046)	(0.085)	(0.076)	(0.092)	(0.103)	(0.021)	(0.112)
Household Assets Index	−0.661***	−1.283***	−1.493***	−1.005***	−0.159***	−0.615***	−0.613***
	(0.019)	(0.039)	(0.061)	(0.172)	(0.022)	(0.030)	(0.055)
Expenditure variables							
The household spends more than it earns	0.253***	0.352***	0.401***	0.272***	0.275***	0.155***	0.203***
	(0.007)	(0.009)	(0.018)	(0.028)	(0.016)	(0.010)	(0.024)
Social programs							
Conditional transfer programs	–	−0.160***	−0.067***	–	–	−0.141***	−0.004
		(0.016)	(0.011)			(0.011)	(0.018)
Labor inclusion programs	–	−0.079*	−0.103***	–	–	−0.041	0.083
		(0.043)	(0.022)			(0.051)	(0.124)
Noncontributory pensions	–	–	−0.148***	–	–	0.036***	–
			(0.056)			(0.009)	
Regional controls	Yes	Yes	Yes	Yes	Yes	Yes	Yes
Observations	51,395	58,817	22,784	1,855	3,893	26,324	6,375

Robust standard errors in parentheses.

*** $p < 0.01$, ** $p < 0.05$, * $p < 0.1$.

Source: Based on household surveys.

Table A.7 Dependent variable: Probability of being subjectively poor, within those households that are not objectively poor.
World Bank poverty line (marginal effects)

	Brazil	Colombia	Ecuador	El Salvador	Paraguay	Peru	Uruguay
Characteristics of the people in the household							
Unemployed head of household	–	0.136***	0.238***	0.081	0.190**	0.079**	0.140***
		(0.025)	(0.058)	(0.372)	(0.080)	(0.031)	(0.042)
Informal head of household	0.024***	0.018*	−0.017	–	−0.018	−0.020***	0.142***
	(0.006)	(0.010)	(0.019)		(0.021)	(0.007)	(0.019)
Presence of a retired person/pensioner in the home	–	−0.072***	−0.002	−0.088	−0.021	0.019*	0.121***
		(0.012)	(0.020)	(0.057)	(0.035)	(0.010)	(0.014)
Head of household with health insurance	−0.126***	−0.042***	−0.137***	–	−0.032	−0.084**	−0.139***
	(0.007)	(0.010)	(0.020)		(0.023)	(0.033)	(0.015)
Immigrant head of household	–	–	−0.121***	0.157	−0.010	–	0.076**
			(0.040)	(0.100)	(0.044)		(0.038)
Housing and household characteristics							
Home tenure (owners)	−0.057***	0.027***	−0.068***	0.024	−0.017	−0.015**	0.041***
	(0.006)	(0.009)	(0.010)	(0.027)	(0.020)	(0.007)	(0.014)
Housing Conditions Index	−0.640***	0.167*	−0.525***	−0.109	−0.839***	−0.151***	−0.880***
	(0.047)	(0.088)	(0.078)	(0.084)	(0.109)	(0.023)	(0.112)
Household Assets Index	−0.676***	−1.317***	−1.518***	−1.785***	−0.229***	−0.582***	−0.631***
	(0.019)	(0.039)	(0.061)	(0.172)	(0.025)	(0.031)	(0.055)

Table A.7 (cont.)

	Brazil	Colombia	Ecuador	El Salvador	Paraguay	Peru	Uruguay
Expenditure variables							
The household spends more than it earns	0.259***	0.378***	0.411***	0.395***	0.393***	0.145***	0.210***
	(0.007)	(0.009)	(0.018)	(0.026)	(0.018)	(0.010)	(0.024)
Social programs							
Conditional transfer programs	–	−0.117***	−0.067***	–	–	−0.143***	0.008
		(0.015)	(0.011)			(0.015)	(0.018)
Labor inclusion programs	–	−0.035	−0.105***	–	–	−0.026	0.065
		(0.040)	(0.023)			(0.053)	(0.123)
Noncontributory pensions	–	–	−0.121**	–	–	0.032***	–
			(0.054)			(0.010)	
Regional controls	Yes	Yes	Yes	Yes	Yes	Yes	Yes
Observations	51,385	64,637	22,822	3,074	4,650	23,606	6,526

Robust standard errors in parentheses.

*** $p < 0.01$, ** $p < 0.05$, * $p < 0.1$.

Source: Based on household surveys.

Table A.8 Dependent variable: Probability of being subjectively poor, within those households that are not objectively poor. National poverty line. Comparison with the inclusion of poverty gap. Marginal effects

	Brazil		Colombia		Ecuador		El Salvador		Paraguay		Peru		Uruguay	
	(1)	(2)	(1)	(2)	(1)	(2)	(1)	(2)	(1)	(2)	(1)	(2)	(1)	(2)
Characteristics of the people in the household														
Unemployed head of household	–	–	0.125***	0.068**	0.253***	0.205***	–	–	0.164**	0.089*	0.083***	0.047*	0.074	−0.016
			(0.028)	(0.026)	(0.058)	(0.058)			(0.068)	(0.046)	(0.032)	(0.026)	(0.046)	(0.024)
Informal head of household	0.012**	−0.004*	0.020*	−0.010	−0.017	−0.020	–	–	−0.029	−0.030**	−0.020***	−0.034***	0.120***	0.040***
	(0.006)	(0.002)	(0.011)	(0.010)	(0.019)	(0.018)			(0.018)	(0.014)	(0.007)	(0.006)	(0.019)	(0.012)
Presence of a retired person/pensioner in the home	–	–	−0.056***	−0.013	−0.003	0.068***	−0.030	−0.012	0.012	0.020	0.019*	0.028***	0.117***	0.060***
			(0.012)	(0.012)	(0.020)	(0.022)	(0.053)	(0.043)	(0.028)	(0.020)	(0.010)	(0.009)	(0.014)	(0.009)
Head of household with health insurance	−0.109***	0.007*	−0.036***	−0.007	−0.139***	−0.056***	–	–	−0.022	−0.016	−0.085**	0.012	−0.106***	−0.008
	(0.007)	(0.003)	(0.011)	(0.010)	(0.020)	(0.019)			(0.019)	(0.015)	(0.036)	(0.035)	(0.015)	(0.009)
Immigrant head of household	–	–	–	–	−0.113***	−0.038	0.076	0.130	0.027	0.032	–	–	0.078**	0.029
					(0.040)	(0.036)	(0.124)	(0.094)	(0.034)	(0.024)			(0.036)	(0.023)
Housing and household characteristics														
Home tenure (owners)	−0.053***	−0.016***	0.031***	0.019**	−0.066***	−0.053***	−0.009	−0.021	−0.033**	−0.044***	−0.014**	−0.018***	0.048***	0.043***
	(0.006)	(0.002)	(0.009)	(0.009)	(0.010)	(0.010)	(0.029)	(0.024)	(0.017)	(0.013)	(0.007)	(0.006)	(0.013)	(0.009)
Housing Conditions Index	−0.730***	−0.505***	0.046	−0.286***	−0.540***	−0.470***	−0.039	0.082	−0.553***	−0.284***	−0.153***	−0.126***	−0.832***	−0.539***
	(0.048)	(0.029)	(0.084)	(0.086)	(0.077)	(0.068)	(0.092)	(0.074)	(0.100)	(0.079)	(0.021)	(0.018)	(0.108)	(0.072)
Household Assets Index	−0.617***	−0.145***	−1.308***	−0.999***	−1.546***	−0.885***	−1.005***	−0.587***	−0.131***	−0.054***	−0.568***	−0.398***	−0.558***	−0.251***
	(0.019)	(0.010)	(0.041)	(0.040)	(0.061)	(0.060)	(0.172)	(0.143)	(0.021)	(0.015)	(0.030)	(0.027)	(0.054)	(0.035)

Table A.8 (cont.)

	Brazil		Colombia		Ecuador		El Salvador		Paraguay		Peru		Uruguay	
	(1)	(2)	(1)	(2)	(1)	(2)	(1)	(2)	(1)	(2)	(1)	(2)	(1)	(2)
Expenditure variables														
The household spends more than it earns	0.230***	0.065***	0.335***	0.262***	0.419***	0.276***	0.272***	0.186***	0.224***	0.109***	0.146***	0.096***	0.176***	0.068***
	(0.007)	(0.004)	(0.010)	(0.010)	(0.018)	(0.016)	(0.028)	(0.025)	(0.016)	(0.018)	(0.010)	(0.008)	(0.024)	(0.015)
Social programs														
Conditional transfer programs	–	–	−0.123***	−0.187***	−0.062***	−0.202***	–	–	–	–	−0.139***	−0.146***	−0.029	−0.119***
			(0.016)	(0.015)	(0.011)	(0.010)					(0.012)	(0.010)	(0.019)	(0.012)
Labor inclusion programs	–	–	−0.066	−0.111**	−0.103***	−0.114***	–	–	–	–	−0.021	−0.021	−0.173	−0.118
			(0.052)	(0.052)	(0.022)	(0.018)					(0.049)	(0.042)	(0.132)	(0.078)
Noncontributory pensions	–	–	–	–	−0.101*	−0.155***	–	–	–	–	0.034***	0.016**	–	–
					(0.054)	(0.045)					(0.009)	(0.008)		
Ratio between Hh income and poverty line		−0.040***		−0.107***		−0.101***		−0.107***		−0.051***		−0.053***		−0.152***
		(0.001)		(0.003)		(0.003)		(0.010)		(0.004)		(0.002)		(0.005)
Regional controls	Yes	Yes	Yes	Yes	Yes	Yes	Yes	Yes	Yes	Yes	Yes	Yes	Yes	Yes
Observations	48,394	48,394	55,508	55,508	23,389	23,389	1,855	1,855	3,527	3,527	24,730	24,730	5,905	5,905

Robust standard errors in parentheses.

*** $p < 0.01$, ** $p < 0.05$, * $p < 0.1$.

Source: Based on household surveys.

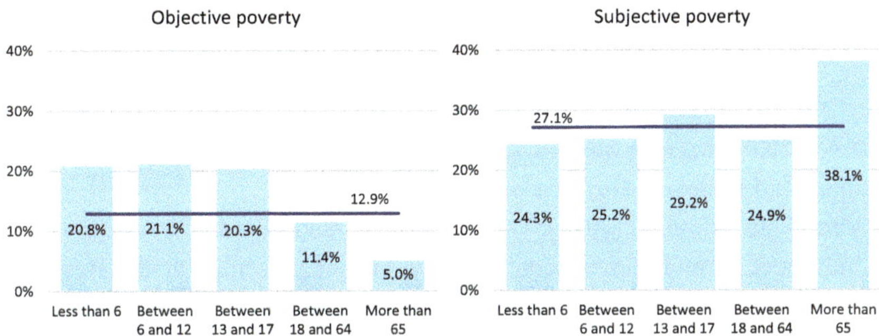

Figure A.1 Objective and Subjective poverty by age group in Uruguay.

Source: Based on Uruguayan household survey.

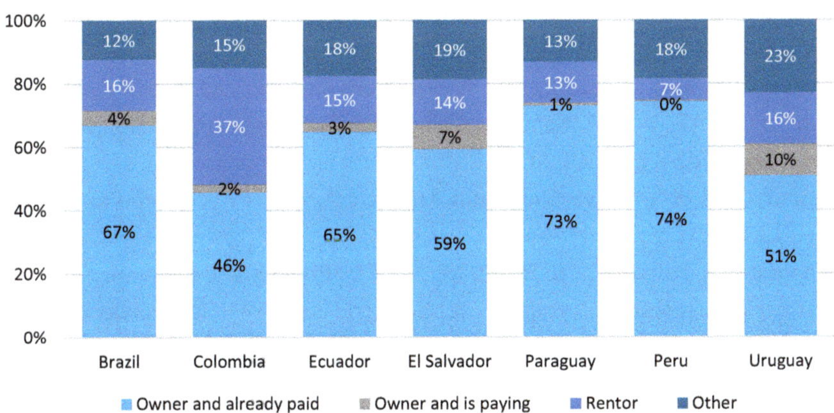

Figure A.2 Home tenure among in Latin America.

Source: Based on household surveys from Brazil (2017–2018), Colombia (2016–2017), Ecuador (2014), El Salvador (2005–2006), Paraguay (2011–2012), Peru (2018), and Uruguay (2016–2017).

References

Alem, Y., Köhlin, G., & Stage, J. (2014). "The persistence of subjective poverty in urban Ethiopia." *World Development*, 56, 51–61.

Alkire, S. & Ballon, P. (2012). "Understanding association across deprivation indicators in multidimensional poverty." Paper presented at the Research Workshop on Dynamic Comparisons between Multidimensional Poverty and Monetary Poverty, Oxford Poverty and Human Development Initiative (OPHI), University of Oxford.

Alkire, S. & Foster, J. (2007). "Counting and multidimensional poverty measurement." *OPHI Working Paper 7*, Oxford University.

Alkire, S. & Foster, J. (2011). "Understandings and misunderstandings of multidimensional poverty measurement." *Journal of Economic Inequality*, 9, 289–314.

Altimir, O. (1979). "La dimensión de la pobreza en América Latina." Cuadernos de la CEPAL, no. 27, Santiago, Economic Commission for Latin America and the Caribbean (ECLAC).

Altimir, O. (1981). "Poverty in Latin America: A review of concepts and data." CEPAL Review, no. 13, 65–91.

Amarante, V., Rossel, C., & Brum, M. (2018). "Poverty and inequality in Latin America's research agenda: A bibliometric review." *Development Policy Review*, 38(4), 465–482.

Arrow, K. (1971). *Essays in the Theory of Risk Bearing*. Amsterdam: North-Holland.

Ayllón, S. & Fusco, A. (2017). "Are income poverty and perceptions of financial difficulties dynamically interrelated?" *Journal of Economic Psychology*, 61, 103–114.

Bertrand, M. & Mullainathan, S. (2001). "Do people mean what they say? Implications for subjective survey data." *The American Economic Review*, 91(2), 67–72.

Besley, T. & Coate, S. (1992). "Understanding welfare stigma: Taxpayer resentment and statistical discrimination." *Journal of Public Economics*, 48(2), 165–183.

Blanchflower, D. & Oswald, A. (2004). "Well-being over time in Britain and the USA." *Journal of Public Economics*, 88, 1359–1386.

Burchardt, T. (2005). "The role of income aspirations in individual happiness." *Social Indicators Research*, 74, 57–104.

Buttler, F. (2013). What determines subjective poverty? An evaluation of the link between relative income poverty measures and subjective economic stress within the EU. DFG Research Unit "Horizontal Europeanization."

Clark, A. (2018). "Four decades of theeEconomics of happiness: Where next?" *The Review of Income and Wealth*, 64(2), 245–269.

Colasanto, D., Kapteyn, A., & Van der Gaag, J. (1984). "Two subjective definitions of poverty: Results from the Wisconsin Basic Needs Study." *The Journal of Human Resources*, 19(1), 127–138.

Danziger, S., Van der Gaag, J., Taussig, M. K., & Smolensky, E. (1984). "The direct measurement of welfare levels: How much does it cost to make ends meet?" *The Review of Economics and Statistics*, 66(3), 500–505.

De Vos, K. & Garner, T. I. (1991). "An evaluation of subjective poverty definitions: Comparing results from the US and the Netherlands." *Review of Income and Wealth*, 37(3), 267–285.

Deaton, A. (1997). *The Analysis of Household Surveys: A Microeconometric Approach to Development Policy*. Baltimore, Maryland: Johns Hopkins University Press.

Deaton, A. (2010). "Price indexes, inequality and the measurement of world poverty." *American Economic Review*, 100(1), 5–34.

Di Tella, R. & MacCulloch, R. (2008). "Gross national happiness as an answer to the Easterlin Paradox?" *Journal of Development Economics*, 86(1), 22–42.

Dolan, P., Peasgood, T., & White, M. (2008). "Do we really know what makes us happy? A review of the economic literature on the factors associated with subjective well-being." *Journal of Economic Psychology*, 29(1), 94–122.

Easterlin, R. (1974). "Does economic growth improve the human lot? Some empirical evidence." In David, R. and Reder, R. (Eds.), *Nations and Households in Economic Growth: Essays in Honor of Moses Abramovitz* (pp. 89–125). New York: Academic Press.

Easterlin, R. A., McVey, L., Switek, M., Sawangfa, O., & Zweig, J. (2010). "The happiness – income paradox revisited." *Proceedings of the National Academy of Sciences*, 107(52), 22463–22468.

ECLAC (2019). *Income Poverty Measurement: Updated Methodology and Results*. ECLAC methodologies. United Nations: Santiago de Chile.

Filandri, M., Pasqua, S., & Struffolino, E. (2020). "Being working poor or feeling working poor? The role of work intensity and job stability for subjective poverty." *Social Indicators Research: An International and Interdisciplinary Journal for Quality of Life Measurement*, 147(3), 781–803.

Flik, R.J. & Van Praag, B. (1991). "Subjective poverty line definitions." *De Economist* 139: 311–330.

Frey, B.S. & Stutzer, A. (2002). "What can economists learn from happiness research?" *Journal of Economic Literature*, vol. 40: 402–435.

Garner, T. I. & de Vos, K. (1995). "Income sufficiency v. poverty: Results from the United States and the Netherlands." *Journal of Population Economics*, 8(2), 117–134.

Garner, T. I. & Short, K. (2003). "Personal assessments of minimum income and expenses: What do they tell us about 'minimum living' thresholds and equivalence scales?" US Department of Labor. *Working Paper 379*.

Gasparini, L., Cicowiez, M., & Sosa Escudero, W. (2013). *Pobreza y Desigualdad en América Latina*. CEDLAS, Universidad Nacional de La Plata.

Goedhart, T., Halberstadt, V., Kapteyn, A., & Van Praag, B. (1977). "The poverty line: Concept and measurement." *Journal of Human Resources*, 12(4), 503–520.

Guagnano, G., Santarelli, E., & Santini, I. (2016). "Can social capital affect subjective poverty in Europe? An empirical analysis based on a generalized ordered logit model." *Social Indicators Research*, 128, 881–907.

Herrera, J. (2002). *La pobreza en el Perú en 2001: Una visión departamental.* Instituto Nacional de Estadística e Informática.

Janský, P. & Kolcunová, D. (2017). "Regional differences in price levels across the European Union and their implications for its regional policy." *The Annals of Regional Science*, 58(3), 641–660.

Jolliffe, D. & Prydz, E. B. (2016). "Estimating international poverty lines from comparable national thresholds." *The Journal of Economic Inequality*, 14(2), 185–198.

Kakwani, N. (2010). "A new model for constructing poverty lines." *Philippine Journal of Development*, 37(2), 35.

Kapteyn, A., Kooreman, P., & Willemse, R. (1988). "Some methodological issues in the implementation of subjective poverty definitions." *The Journal of Human Resources*, 22(2), 222–242.

Li, S. & Cai, M. (2024). "Social support and reference group: The dual action mechanism of the social network on subjective poverty." *Humanities and Social Sciences Communications*, 11, 349.

Lokshin, M., Umapathi, N., & Paternostro, S. (2006). "Robustness of subjective welfare analysis in a poor developing country: Madagascar 2001." *The Journal of Development Studies*, 42(4), 559–591.

Lucchetti, L. (2006). "Caracterización de la percepción del bienestar y cálculo de la línea de pobreza subjetiva en Argentina." CEDLAS, Universidad Nacional de La Plata.

Mahmood, T., Yu, X., & Klasen, S. (2019). "Do the poor really feel poor? Comparing objective poverty with subjective poverty in Pakistan." *Social Indicators Research*, 142(2), 543–580.

Maruejols, L., Wang, H., Zhao, Q., Bai, Y., & Zhang, L. (2022). "Comparison of machine learning predictions of subjective poverty in rural China." *China Agricultural Economic Review*, 15(2), 379–399.

Monge, A. & Winkelried, Q. (2001). "Consideraciones subjetivas en la medición de la pobreza en el Perú. Apuntes." *Revista De Ciencias Sociales*, 48, 129–170.

Niño-Muñoz, D. (2023). "Institutional development in main Colombian cities: What is its relation to subjective poverty?" *Latin American Research Review*, 58(4), 837–857.

Noll, H. & Weick, S. (2015). "Consumption expenditures and subjective well-being: Empirical evidence from Germany." *International Review of Economics*, 62(2), 101–119.

Oishi, S. & Kesebir, S. (2015). "Income inequality explains why economic growth does not always translate to an increase in happiness." *Psychological Science*, 26(10), 1630–1638.

Orshansky, M. (1965). "Counting the poor: Another look at the poverty profile." *Social Security Bulletin*, 28, 3–29.

Ortiz-Pech, R., Alvarez -Marchan, G., & Albornoz-Mendoza, L. (2019). "Pobreza objetiva y subjetiva de los hogares en Timul, Yucatán, y su dependencia a programas sociales." *Estudios Sociales*, 29(54), 4–29.

Peng, C. (2021). "What makes people feel poor when they are economically non-poor? Investigating the role of intergenerational mobility and comparison with friends." *Research in Social Stratification and Mobility*, 75, 100645.

Peng, C. (2023). "Household consumption and the discrepancy between economic and subjective poverty: The mediating roles of perceived social status and social connectedness." *Journal of Happiness Studies*, 24(5), 1703–1727.

Peng, C. & Law, Y. W. (2023). "How do consumption patterns influence the discrepancy between economic and subjective poverty?," *Journal of Happiness Studies*, 24(4), 1579–1604.

Peng, C. & Yip, P. (2023). "Access to neighbourhood services and subjective poverty in Hong Kong." *Applied Research in Quality of Life*, 18(2), 1015–1035.

Peng, C., Yip, P. S. F., & Law, Y. W. (2020). "What factors beyond economic poverty lead people in high-income societies to feel poor? Evidence from Hong Kong." *Social Indicators Research*, 152, 991–1027.

Pinzon Gutiérrez, L. F. (2017). "Factores asociados a la pobreza subjetiva en Colombia: un estudio desde el enfoque de las capacidades y la economía de la felicidad." *Revista Desarrollo y Sociedad*, 1(78), 11–57.

Posel, D. & Rogan, M. (2014). "Measured as por versus feeling poor: Comparing money-metric and subjective poverty rates in South Africa." *Journal of Human Development and Capabilities*, 17(1): 55–73.

Pradhan, M. & Ravallion, M. (2000). "Measuring poverty using qualitative perceptions of consumption adequacy." *Review of Economics and Statistics*, 82(3), 462–471.

Ravallion, M. (2010). "Poverty lines across the world." Policy Research Working Paper Series 5284, The World Bank.

Ravallion, M. (2012). "Poor, or just feeling poor? On using subjective data in measuring poverty." Policy Research Working Paper Series 5968, The World Bank.

Ravallion, M. (2016). *The Economics of Poverty: History, Measurement and Policy*. New York: Oxford University Press.

Ravallion, M., Datt, G., & Walle, D. (1991). "Quantifying absolute poverty in the developing world." *Review of Income and Wealth*, 37(4), 345–361.

Ravallion, M. & Lokshin, M. (2001). "Identifying welfare effects from subjective questions." *Economica*, 68, 335–357.

Ravallion, M. & Lokshin, M. (2002). "Self-rated economic welfare in Russia." *European Economic Review*, 46(8), 1453–1473.

Roelen, K. (2020). "Receiving social assistance in low- and middle-income countries: Negating shame or producing stigma?" *Journal of Social Policy*, 49(4), 705–723.

Rojas, M. & Jiménez, E. (2008). "Pobreza subjetiva en México: el papel de las normas de evaluación del ingreso." *Perfiles latinoamericanos*, 16(32), 11–33.

Ruggeri Laderchi, C., Saith, R., & Stewart, F. (2003). "Does it Matter that we do not Agree on the Definition of Poverty? A Comparison of Four Approaches." *Oxford Development Studies*, 31(3), 243–274.

Santos, M. E. & Villatoro, P. (2018). "A multidimensional poverty index for Latin America." *Review of Income and Wealth*, 64(1), 52–82.

Scalese, F. (2022). "Pobreza subjetiva: una primera aproximación para el caso uruguayo." Serie Documentos de investigación estudiantil, DIE 02/2022. Instituto de Economía, Facultad de Ciencias Económicas y Administración, Universidad de la República, Uruguay.

Seidl, C. (1994). "How sensible is the Leyden individual welfare function of income?" *European Economic Review*, 38(8), 1633–1659.

Sen, A. (1985). *Commodities and Capabilities*. Amsterdam: North-Holland.

Shucksmith, M., Cameron, S., Merridew, T., & Pichler, F. (2009). "Urban – rural differences in quality of life across the European Union." *Regional Studies*, 43(10), 1275–1289.

Tobasura, E. & Casas, J. (2017). "La línea de pobreza subjetiva para Tunja, Colombia." *Revista Apuntes del CENES*, 36(64), 253–282.

Van Praag, B. & Ferrer-i-Carbonell, A. (2004). "Happiness quantified: A satisfaction calculus approach." *The Journal of Economic Inequality*, 4(3), 391–395.

Van Praag, B. & Ferrer-i-Carbonell, A. (2005). *Happiness Quantified: A Satisfaction Calculus Approach*, 1st Ed., Oxford: Oxford University Press.

Van Praag, B., Goedhart, T., & Kapteyn, A. (1980). "The poverty line – a pilot survey in Europe." *The Review of Economics and Statistics*, 62(3), 461–465.

Van Praag, B. & Kapteyn, A. (1973). "Further evidence on the individual welfare function of income: An empirical investigation in the Netherlands." *European Economic Review*, 4, 33–62.

Van Praag, B. & Kapteyn, A. (1994). "How sensible is the Leyden individual welfare function of income? A reply." *European Economic Review*, 38(9), 1817–1825.

Van Praag, B. M. (1968). *Individual Welfare Functions and Consumer Behavior: A Theory of Rational Irrationality* (Vol. 57). North-Holland.

Van Praag, B. M. (1971). "The welfare function of income in Belgium: An empirical investigation." *European Economic Review*, 2(3), 337–369.

Van Praag, B. M., Spit, J. S., & Van de Stadt, H. (1982). "A comparison between the food ratio poverty line and the Leyden poverty line." *The Review of Economics and Statistics*, 64(4), 691–694.

Wang, H., Zhao, Q., Bai, Y., Zhang, L., & Yu, X. (2020). "Poverty and subjective poverty in rural China." *Social Indicators Research*, 150(1), 219–242.

Želinský, T., Mysíková, M., & Garner, T. I. (2022). "Trends in subjective income poverty rates in the European Union." *European Journal of Development Review*, 34, 2493–2516.

Cambridge Elements ≡

Development Economics

Series Editor-in-Chief

Kunal Sen
UNU-WIDER and University of Manchester

Kunal Sen, UNU-WIDER Director, is Editor-in-Chief of the Cambridge Elements in Development Economics series. Professor Sen has over three decades of experience in academic and applied development economics research, and has carried out extensive work on international finance, the political economy of inclusive growth, the dynamics of poverty, social exclusion, female labour force participation, and the informal sector in developing economies. His research has focused on India, East Asia, and sub-Saharan Africa.

In addition to his work as Professor of Development Economics at the University of Manchester, Kunal has been the Joint Research Director of the Effective States and Inclusive Development (ESID) Research Centre, and a Research Fellow at the Institute for Labor Economics (IZA). He has also served in advisory roles with national governments and bilateral and multilateral development agencies, including the UK's Department for International Development, Asian Development Bank, and the International Development Research Centre.

Thematic Editors

Tony Addison
University of Copenhagen and UNU-WIDER

Tony Addison is a Professor of Economics in the University of Copenhagen's Development Economics Research Group. He is also a Non-Resident Senior Research Fellow at UNU-WIDER, Helsinki, where he was previously the Chief Economist-Deputy Director. In addition, he is Professor of Development Studies at the University of Manchester. His research interests focus on the extractive industries, energy transition, and macroeconomic policy for development.

Chris Barrett
SC Johnson College of Business, Cornell University

Chris Barrett is an agricultural and development economist at Cornell University. He is the Stephen B. and Janice G. Ashley Professor of Applied Economics and Management; and International Professor of Agriculture at the Charles H. Dyson School of Applied Economics and Management. He is also an elected Fellow of the American Association for the Advancement of Science, the Agricultural and Applied Economics Association, and the African Association of Agricultural Economists.

Carlos Gradín
University of Vigo

Carlos Gradín is a professor of applied economics at the University of Vigo. His main research interest is the study of inequalities, with special attention to those that exist between population groups (e.g., by race or sex). His publications have contributed to improving the empirical evidence in developing and developed countries, as well as globally, and to improving the available data and methods used.

Rachel M. Gisselquist

UNU-WIDER

Rachel M. Gisselquist is a Senior Research Fellow and member of the Senior Management Team of UNU-WIDER. She specializes in the comparative politics of developing countries, with particular attention to issues of inequality, ethnic and identity politics, foreign aid and state building, democracy and governance, and sub-Saharan African politics. Dr Gisselquist has edited a dozen collections in these areas, and her articles are published in a range of leading journals.

Shareen Joshi

Georgetown University

Shareen Joshi is an Associate Professor of International Development at Georgetown University's School of Foreign Service in the United States. Her research focuses on issues of inequality, human capital investment and grassroots collective action in South Asia. Her work has been published in the fields of development economics, population studies, environmental studies and gender studies.

Patricia Justino

UNU-WIDER and IDS – UK

Patricia Justino is a Senior Research Fellow at UNU-WIDER and Professorial Fellow at the Institute of Development Studies (IDS) (on leave). Her research focuses on the relationship between political violence, governance and development outcomes. She has published widely in the fields of development economics and political economy and is the co-founder and co-director of the Households in Conflict Network (HiCN).

Marinella Leone

University of Pavia

Marinella Leone is an assistant professor at the Department of Economics and Management, University of Pavia, Italy. She is an applied development economist. Her more recent research focuses on the study of early child development parenting programmes, on education, and gender-based violence. In previous research she investigated the short-, long-term and intergenerational impact of conflicts on health, education and domestic violence. She has published in top journals in economics and development economics.

Jukka Pirttilä

University of Helsinki and UNU-WIDER

Jukka Pirttilä is Professor of Public Economics at the University of Helsinki and VATT Institute for Economic Research. He is also a Non-Resident Senior Research Fellow at UNU-WIDER. His research focuses on tax policy, especially for developing countries. He is a co-principal investigator at the Finnish Centre of Excellence in Tax Systems Research.

Andy Sumner

King's College London and UNU-WIDER

Andy Sumner is Professor of International Development at King's College London; a Non-Resident Senior Fellow at UNU-WIDER and a Fellow of the Academy of Social Sciences. He has published extensively in the areas of poverty, inequality, and economic development.

Cambridge Elements⁼

Development Economics

Elements in the Series

Parental Investments and Children's Human Capital in Low-to-Middle-Income Countries
Jere R. Behrman

Great Gatsby and the Global South: Intergenerational Mobility, Income Inequality, and Development
Diding Sakri, Andy Sumner and Arief Anshory Yusuf

Varieties of Structural Transformation: Patterns, Determinants, and Consequences
Kunal Sen

Economic Transformation and Income Distribution in China over Three Decades
Cai Meng, Bjorn Gustafsson and John Knight

Chilean Economic Development under Neoliberalism: Structural Transformation, High Inequality and Environmental Fragility
Andrés Solimano and Gabriela Zapata-Román

Hierarchy of Needs and the Measurement of Poverty and Standards of Living
Joseph Deutsch and Jacques Silber

New Structural Financial Economics: A Framework for Rethinking the Role of Finance in Serving the Real Economy
Justin Yifu Lin, Jiajun Xu, Zirong Yang and Yilin Zhang

Knowledge and Global Inequality Since 1800: Interrogating the Present as History
Dev Nathan

Survival of the Greenest: Economic Transformation in a Climate-conscious World
Amir Lebdioui

Escaping Poverty Traps and Unlocking Prosperity in the Face of Climate Risk: Lessons from Index-Based Livestock Insurance
Nathaniel D. Jensen, Francesco P. Fava, Andrew G. Mude, Christopher B. Barrett, Brenda Wandera-Gache, Anton Vrieling, Masresha Taye, Kazushi Takahashi, Felix Lung, Munenobu Ikegami, Polly Ericksen, Philemon Chelanga, Sommarat Chantarat, Michael Carter, Hassan Bashir and Rupsha Banerjee

Financing for Development: The Global Agenda
José Antonio Ocampo

Poverty in Latin America: Feelings/Perceptions vs Material Conditions
Verónica Amarante, Maira Colacce and Federico Scalese

A full series listing is available at: www.cambridge.org/CEDE

For EU product safety concerns, contact us at Calle de José Abascal, 56–1°,
28003 Madrid, Spain or eugpsr@cambridge.org.

www.ingramcontent.com/pod-product-compliance
Ingram Content Group UK Ltd.
Pitfield, Milton Keynes, MK11 3LW, UK
UKHW021307100625
459283UK00039B/170